RISE

RISE

3 PRACTICAL STEPS FOR

Advancing Your Career,
Standing Out as a Leader,
AND LIKING YOUR LIFE

PATTY AZZARELLO

Foreword by Keith Ferrazzi

TEN SPEED PRESS
Berkeley

Ten Speed Press and the Ten Speed Press colophon are registered trademarks
of Random House, Inc.

Originally published in the United States in somewhat different form as
Rise: How to Be Really Successful at Work AND Like Your Life by Newton
Park Publishing, Palo Alto, California, in 2010.

Back cover author photo copyright © 2011 by Anne Knudsen.
Author photo on page 271 copyright © 2010 by Pacific Media.

Library of Congress Cataloging-in-Publication Data
Azzarello, Patty.
   Rise : 3 practical steps for advancing your career, standing out as a leader,
and liking your life / by Patty Azzarello ; foreword by Keith Ferrazzi. — 1st
Ten Speed ed.
      p. cm.
   Rev. ed. of: Rise : how to be really successful at work and like your life.
Newtown Park Pub., c2011.
   Includes index.
   Summary: "A successful Silicon Valley executive and consultant shares
straight-shooting advice for succeeding at work without losing your sanity
in three steps: do better, look better, and connect better"—Provided by
publisher.
1. Success in business. 2. Career development. I. Title.
   HF5386.A99 2012
   650.1—dc23
                                2011051574
ISBN 978-1-60774-260-9
eISBN 978-1-60774-261-6

Printed in the United States of America on recycled paper (20% PCW)

Design by Katy Brown

20 19 18 17 16 15 14 13

First Ten Speed Press Edition

Thank You.

To the people who genuinely helped me learn the most important lessons in work and life, in order of appearance: Mom, Dad, Kerry, Al, Jim, Jacek, and Nick.

To the many people who personally went out of their way to help me succeed: You are too numerous to list.

Contents

Part 3
CONNECT Better—Get Support

BUILDING CONNECTIONS

LANDING THE BIG JOB

Part 4
GO!—Make Your Work, and Your Life, Work

Foreword

I tasted corporate success early. Two of my first major career achievements (partner at Deloitte and Fortune 500 CMO) won me the right to call myself "the youngest *x*" in my early professional bio. And so I smiled as I read Patty's bio for this book: "Patty Azzarello became the youngest general manager at Hewlett-Packard at age thirty-three, ran a $1 billion software business at thirty-five, and became a CEO at thirty-eight (without turning into a self-centered, miserable jerk)."

See also *Rise*'s subtitle, which addresses both career advancement *and* liking your life. Patty is starting everyone who is reading this book off on the right foot by admitting that yes, there is a tension between radical success and personal happiness, and yes, it *is* reconcilable—provided that your success strategy is designed with that in mind. By showing you how to plot your own course for success, by engineering the right combination of what your company values and what best leverages your natural strengths, *Rise* gives you the tools and insights you need to make it happen.

Man, is this book ever needed. Corporate America has by and large done a poor job helping workers be both ambitious and collaborative, successful and happy. One need only look at the October 2011 Gallup report showing that more than 70 percent of American workers are disengaged or even "actively disengaged" for evidence.

I've often said that I wish I had written my second book, *Who's Got Your Back*, before my first book, *Never Eat Alone*—or at least that people would read them in that order. *Who's Got Your Back* was the manual I wished I'd had to help me navigate the incredible success sparked by my fast corporate climb and the spark (explosion, really) of *Never Eat Alone*. It was the book I wrote after learning how to create an inner circle of relationships that would allow me to best discover, as Bill George would say, "my true North," and really leverage every opportunity my success created. And in some regards, it was the book I wrote to make sure I (and others) didn't turn into "self-centered, miserable jerks."

Readers of *Rise* won't have to worry about that. Patty never forgets that success is about more than incremental or even stratospheric gains in your career; it's about enjoying your work and nurturing the relationships you make along the way. She recognizes that the most efficacious "corporate power grabs" aren't those that pit you against the people around you but those that draw them into a shared collaborative vision. To be a leader is not just to find solutions but specifically to find those that help build, strengthen, and expand your team.

To give just one example, I love Patty's recognition that diligently creating a strong network of relationships means that *anyone* is a potential project resource, not just your direct reports. When you make a conscious decision to "connect better" (step 3 in Patty's strategic map) you have access to intelligent resources that your counterparts do not. People are happy to help you out—it doesn't have to be in their job description. They're hungry to be on your team, and stuff gets done.

I always say that you need to start every day, every event, every meeting with the same two goals: Find a way to help and find a way to care. Care about what you're doing and care about the people you're doing it with. This book serves up a powerful course of action that will keep you true to both those intentions so that both extraordinary success *and* life satisfaction can be yours.

—Keith Ferrazzi, founder and CEO, Ferrazzi Greenlight, Inc., and author of *Never Eat Alone* and *Who's Got Your Back*

Working versus Succeeding

I have always been fascinated with really successful people. What actually got them to the top? Was it *being really good at what they do* that set them apart? Or was there more to it?

It struck me that big success did not just happen unexpectedly to talented, fortunate people. And it didn't happen to the people who tirelessly worked really hard at their jobs.

Highly successful people seemed to get there by breaking through limitations of how their jobs were defined—by conceiving and doing extra things above and around their job descriptions.

The most successful people have some other things in common:

- Yes, they are really good at what they do, but what they are doing seems to suit them personally. They are truly being themselves.

- They stand out as being different from their peers. They are not doing their job *as written*—and they always get bigger results with a wider impact than everyone around them.

- They have amazing networks of people they can go to for information and help. In fact, getting help is something they do regularly.

- They command immense respect from others.

- They fail more than most people. They hear "no" a lot. They screw up. But they get up again. They learn. They keep going.

- They DO stuff. It's not always dramatic, but there is always a sense that they are taking action and making steady forward progress.

- Most of them have plenty of money, but that was never the whole point for them. They seem genuinely satisfied with their lives. They have happy families, take vacations, and even enjoy hobbies and community interests.

I also met many rich people who were miserable and many successful people who were complete jerks, but they didn't fit my definition of "success," so I didn't include them in my model!

Why I Wrote This Book

I wrote the book that I wished I had been able to read as I was building my own career. I want to help people get further, faster, and be more satisfied with their work. There were four real motivators for the book.

1. Tell All the Secrets

I was very fortunate to get a lot of help from smart people who cared about me along the way. Because of that, I was told a lot of important things that no one else was. Without executive-level, personal mentors, most people don't ever get to learn about what really matters and what really works. They don't learn how to avoid the common pitfalls or get the insights they need to survive the confusing and rough times.

So I want to give away all the secrets—all the executive, insider information that is typically shared with only a select few people who get taken under a mentor's wing.

2. I Hate Wasted Time

I hate wasting anything, particularly time, energy, and potential. So I don't like to see people wasting time, investing their heart and energy, but not getting anywhere—and, in fact, burning career capital.

You see, I am a maximizer through and through. What I mean by that is that I am driven to find the most direct and effective path to accomplish things and then do them the best they can be done, whether that is being a CEO or making a tuna sandwich.

As such, I invest enormous amounts of time, thought, and energy to figure out how to do something an easier, faster, or better way. I refuse to let my time get burned up on things that don't make a big difference or have a significant payoff. So I've spent a lot of the last twenty-five years figuring out how to tune my actions and invest my efforts to maximize the payoff for the businesses *and* for my career.

I know what works. I got there. I know how you can get the career *you* want. Through all my learning, mistakes, failures, embarrassments, wins, and advances (and maximizing) along the way, I've broken the code. I have defined and developed a concrete, practical, and repeatable approach for building the success you want. I've learned how to benefit both my business and my career and not get killed in the process. And I want to share how you can do it, too.

3. It's OK to Take Care of Yourself

I want to help people recognize that taking care of your career is not selfish. When you start managing your career on purpose, you end up doing a better job because *in order to advance your career, you must add more value to the business.* In fact, adding more value is the only reliable way to advance. So taking control of your career is not just good for you; your team and your company also benefit because you become more capable and more valuable. Conversely, if you never focus on taking care of yourself, you will get buried with work, burned out, and used up and you'll miss the chance to grow.

4. You Can Get There

It has been a huge lesson for me that breakout success can come from doing relatively simple things. The key is in the *doing.* And the things that have the biggest impact are all very doable; the problem is that they are easy to miss if you don't learn them and if you don't make it a point to do them on purpose.

My Repeatable Approach for Success

It's not that the unspoken rules of success are any big secret; it's just that most executives never bother to talk about them or share them in a way that is useful to and doable by others. That's where this book and the model I have developed come in.

I want to give you big insights that will shape how you think about your work for the rest of your life, and practical ideas for things you can start doing right now that will make a big difference in your success.

In this book I have gathered all the ideas, insights, and necessary actions and provided the context for how it all works together. Success doesn't come from being good at just one thing. It comes from doing a combination of things on purpose, over time, that all build on each other to create remarkable outcomes. But you have to understand the whole picture to know why each part of it matters.

My approach for success has three parts. I am a pretty plainspoken person, so I call them

- DO Better

- LOOK Better

- CONNECT Better

Big success requires all three—not in isolation or in sequence, but in combination. Missing any one of them is what causes most career stalls or washouts. Without taking some care to make progress on all three, you fall behind—you get stuck.

Here is where you can begin to see why hard work alone doesn't cut it. The work is only in the DO Better category. If you burn up all your time and energy doing excellent work, you may fail to get recognized (LOOK Better) and fail to build a network of support (CONNECT Better). So your career stalls. You are doing an excellent job of everything that is asked of you but you still get stuck.

Remember, it's not just about the work.

To add real value to the business, you need to understand what is truly valuable to the business and you need to build a broad network of support so you can deliver significant results in a big and far-reaching enough way.

DO Better

DO Better is about producing exceptional results. DO Better is about working on the right things in the right ways. It's about rising above the work. DO Better is about freeing yourself from your overwhelming tactical workload and identifying and delivering on the few most critical outcomes—the ones that really count. DO Better is about tuning your job, knowing yourself really well, and putting yourself in situations where you can thrive in your work and accomplish exceptional things. It's also about how you lead, build trust, delegate, make more time, and build up your energy. Successful people are not burned out and used up. And they are not the ones who were less busy along the way. They deliver remarkable results and leave room to DO even better after that.

LOOK Better

LOOK Better is about standing out. Successful people do their work and produce their results in a way that is meaningful and visible to people that count. They understand which audiences matter most and they communicate with the right people at the right times, in a compelling way.

LOOK Better is about building personal and professional credibility and becoming more relevant with your key stakeholders. People with high credibility get more done because they face fewer obstacles. Successful people are widely known not just for doing their jobs really well, but for the extra value they contribute to the business. They have risen above the work and proven their greater, wider-reaching value to their companies.

CONNECT Better

The most successful people get a lot of help. CONNECT Better is about building a broad base of support for yourself, your team, and your work. As you advance, your focus needs to broaden, not deepen.

Successful people are not isolated in their own world. They build the right networks of mentors, partners, and supporters. They know how to get on "the List" of people who get access to the best opportunities.

It's not about politics; it's about effectiveness. Successful people build an "extra team" around them and accomplish big things by working with and through others. The higher you go, the more your value is associated with your network.

It's Never Too Early to Begin or Too Late to Start

There are no prerequisites, hurdles, or qualifications to using the model. Set your sights on adding more value to the business and start from where you are today.

You Have More Control Than You Think

You need to recognize that it is up to you to make things happen in your career, without counting on standard company and management processes. These days, if anything, the standard company and management processes are set against you!

My approach is all about the things *you* can control—how to see them and how to act on them. You need to do specific things on purpose in all three areas of DO Better, LOOK Better, and CONNECT Better over time.

For example, working really hard won't get you anywhere if no one sees what you are doing or if they think it's irrelevant. Creating a publicity campaign without the results to back it up will backfire. (We all know those people who are managing their publicity instead of doing their jobs, and it's hard not to wish bad things for them.)

You can't build a strong network if you are not credible, and you won't know how to use contributions from your network if you are not focused on doing the most critical few things to move the business forward. It all works together to add value and grow success in your business and career.

The real payoff comes over time—once you feel like you have mastered all three, you set the bar higher—and do them all again. That's where the "better" comes in.

I Learned the Hard Way

Here's an example of how this works and what happens if you miss the boat—like I did.

In my late twenties I got my first top management role, running a software development organization for a major corporation.

In my first year in that role, I turned around the struggling organization. I built a team that achieved stellar results. We cut the time it took to develop a product in half. We released a higher-quality product on time (on the new shorter development calendar). We won the sales force back (they had abandoned us due to lack of confidence). We significantly improved team morale and restored customer satisfaction.

I thought, "Not bad for a year's work!" It was a lot to get done in one year. It stood out. I felt very proud (and very tired!).

Great Work Was Not Enough

Alas, I had nailed only the DO Better part.

Up until then, I had operated with the understanding that if you deliver great results, you get recognition and rewards. The annual review/raise cycle coincided with my one-year anniversary. The company was doing well. I had given generous pay raises to my top performers, and I was excited to have the conversation with my boss about my pay raise—but I got a rude awakening.

When we had that conversation, I learned that I got no raise—zero. He agreed that I had exceeded expectations and he thanked me for what I had accomplished, so I asked him, "What happened?"

Nobody Knows You

"Nobody knows you," he replied. "I tried, but nobody knows you."*

"What does that have to do with anything?!!" [Surprise. Anger. Bewilderment!]

This was indeed a rude awakening. Not only was good work not enough—great work and great results were not enough!

Alas, I had missed LOOK Better entirely. No one outside of my own organization or my boss knew what I had accomplished. That's how I learned that many people in addition to my boss got a say in what happened to me. Oops.

Thus began my journey to learn about all the other stuff you need to do, in addition to exceeding your job description, to get ahead.

I began to focus on the LOOK Better part, building my visibility with the people who counted. I began to seek out and communicate with key executives across the company. I began to understand what they really cared about and I tried to find ways to make my work relevant to them. This required a significant effort. So I first had to go back to DO Better and do *even better* than I was doing before—I still needed to deliver outstanding results but in a new way so that I could make room to do the extra things I needed to do to LOOK Better.

I began to see results from my LOOK Better effort. I was building credibility, and my team was getting recognized for our good work. In fact, our work in reducing product development time and improving quality was so admired that I began to get asked to speak to other organizations to share how we did it. Although that was a big boost to my LOOK Better efforts, it's important to note that this never would have happened if we hadn't delivered the outstanding results in the first place—the DO Better part. Doing exceptional work is what gives you something real to create visibility for. They go together.

Over the next couple of years, though, I felt my career stall again. What was missing? CONNECT Better. I had not been building my network and my "extra team"—the group of people outside my organization, in other groups and at other levels, who could provide additional support. As great and as visible as my results were, I was not seen as being ready for something bigger because I was not influencing the business outside my own business unit.

---

*My manager in this case was actually pretty awesome, even though this is a sad part of the story. He did three things at this point:
  1. He went to bat for me again and got me a small raise right away.
  2. He taught me the value of being positive and patient and of seeing the opportunity I had ahead of me instead of getting pissed off and blowing it.
  3. He really helped me build my network so this would not happen again and he taught me the value of doing so.

Ultimately, I struck gold on CONNECT Better with mentors. In fact, aside from my own efforts, mentors had a bigger impact on my success, by far, than anything else. Mentors help you connect at levels and places you would never connect with on your own. Successful people build networks, get help, and have mentors.

The Moral of the Story

As you advance in a company, success becomes less about the specific work you do and more about who you are as a person and a leader. It's about your ability to create broad visibility, credibility, connections, and support outside your organization. The higher you go, the more your results come from enabling people who work for you to deliver great things *and* from working with people around and above you to eliminate obstacles, get ideas, negotiate for resources, secure cooperation, and build momentum on a large scale. It's not about the work you deliver personally.

Where I Came From

Growing up, I was a fat kid and a nerd. I was an artist, a singer, and an actor, and I was drawn to math and science.

When I started at university, I was registered as a fine arts major, but when I showed up at orientation I heard my mother's voice in my head saying (for as far back as I could remember), "You will go to college. You will get a good education and a good job and you will support yourself. Never rely on anyone else to support you. That's your job."

So, fearing I would struggle to earn a good living as an artist, I crossed out "Fine arts," penciled in "Electronic engineering," and went to stand in the electronic engineering line.

After college, I began my career at Bell Labs in Holmdel, New Jersey, as an engineer in the robotics research lab. I hated it. I was miserable and thought I had screwed up my life (more on this and what I did about it later).

I went on to work in individual roles as a technical sales consultant, a sales rep, a product manager, and a product marketing manager. I did plenty of trade show booth duty. I know what it's like to start in a thankless, entry-level job.

In my late twenties I got my first big multilevel management job running a software development organization of about 150 people. I eventually held executive roles in marketing and sales organizations as well as general management.

My career really took off when I became Hewlett Packard's youngest general manager at the age of thirty-three. I was running a $1 billion software business for HP at thirty-five and was CEO of a private software company at thirty-eight.

I am very lucky to still have the guidance of many mentors and brilliant people who care about me. I could not have achieved any level of success without the support of my parents, sister, and husband. I still enjoy art and I'm an avid cyclist and scuba diver. I donate to charities and I like expensive shoes. I am no longer fat but I am still kind of a nerd.

What Is Here for You in This Book

1. **Insights**
   - I include all the unspoken rules and secrets I have uncovered along the way.
   - I describe what counts most toward building real success, and which common hazards and traps are a waste of time or can get you blacklisted.
   - *Key insights*—I call these out as the big ideas. Once you learn them, they create a permanent improvement in your career and life.

2. **My Repeatable Approach for Success**
   - The book is organized into the three sections of my approach: DO Better, LOOK Better, and CONNECT Better. You will learn how to become better in each of these areas and you'll learn why it matters so much.
   - The model contains key insights that will change the way you view your success and your ability to make it happen.
   - The model contains practical ideas and useful suggestions for things you can do *now*, on purpose, that will have a dramatic effect on your success.

3. **Resources**
   - I supply pointers to important and useful resources I have found most helpful along the way.
   - I share my recipe for a tuna sandwich.

Who Should Read This Book?

Managers—don't try advancing in a corporation without reading this book! It will help you get there much faster and with less pain.

If you are already an executive, you will get important ideas for developing your leaders—and your life will get easier when your whole team reads it.

If you don't manage people, you'll get lots of practical ideas to increase your effectiveness and preserve your value. You'll also gain valuable insight into what managers worry about, which will help you do your job better and get more recognition.

And anyone in search of a job, a promotion, or a new customer will get strategies to optimize what you deliver and how you are perceived.

Part 1

DO Better

Have More Impact

Learn the vital difference between
working hard and succeeding.
Deal with frustrating obstacles
and stupid people.

1. Be Less Busy

Productive Laziness

OK, here's the rub.

Before we even get started on the DO Better part of the model, you can imagine that throughout this book I'm going to suggest that you do things you are not doing today. But if you are like most people, you have no extra time.

The key point: You need to have time to do extra things. If you don't make yourself less busy, it's game over. You might as well put this book down and just go back to work.

You need to use your time differently. You need to rise above the work. You need to figure out how to make yourself less busy with your current workload to make room to do higher-value work. No one will do this for you.

The Overbusy Manifesto

No one other than YOU has any motivation whatsoever to make you less busy. Your team, your boss, your peers, and your business partners only benefit from your tireless output.

If you are overwhelmed by the activities of your job and you use up all your time and energy on your current job, you are not ready for a bigger one. Simple as that.

The most successful people are not the ones who were less busy along the way. They weren't given more time to be strategic and more room in their schedule to add more value. They figured out how to do it anyway.

Embrace Your Inner Laziness

The first thing you need to do is to give yourself permission to be less busy.

> **KEY INSIGHT:** *It's important to realize that not only do you have permission, but also as a leader you are expected to be able to deal with an overwhelming workload and not be overwhelmed. That's the job.*

Your job as a leader is to deal with chaos and pressure and make it more manageable. You are supposed to create systems and processes to get more done with less effort. You are expected to think strategically, prioritize, and focus on the most critical tasks. But you'll never get to do any of this if you don't first give yourself permission to be less busy.

No One Cares How Hard You Work

No one will discover or promote you for being a hard worker. It's up to you (not your manager or your company) to reinvent your job so that you can work where the value is. And when you do that, working gets easier. You suffer less and accomplish more—for your business and your career.

It Can Be Scary to Stop

Many people feel that if they are not fully consumed with work and always appearing to be super busy, people will question their commitment and their value. It's as if their stopping to take some time to think will make others think they are not doing anything.

Delivering Work Is Not the Same Thing as Adding Value

This is a really important point. If you don't internalize this point, you will get stuck. Never confuse *output* with *outcome*.

Think about it this way. When you start out in an entry-level position, your job is to do work. You might be writing, testing, selling, or building; whatever the task, you can think of the value you deliver to your company as directly tied to the time you put in. If you take an extra hour for lunch, you are stealing an hour of value away from your company.

But when you are a manager, the value you add to your company is no longer based on the hours you spend at work. It is based on the value of the outcomes you create. If you take an extra hour for lunch and take a walk, and you return with a new idea to improve the efficiency of your team by 20 percent, you've added more than one hour of value. If you think of a new marketing approach or customer service offering that increases revenue, or you solve a persistent issue that is holding up your team or business, not only are you not stealing an hour from the company, but you are also building value.

On the other hand, if you never take that hour and you stay busy with tactical activities, you may have put in your time and looked busy (delivered lots of output), but you are not creating value (outcomes) by helping the company get the work done in a more efficient or more effective way.

The Most Effective Leaders Have Mastered a Useful Kind of Selfishness and Laziness

Selfishness: "I can't keep working like this. I am suffering. I'm not OK working like this forever. I need to find a way to change this so I can be happier and more satisfied with what I am doing."

Laziness: "This is just too hard. The payoff is not worth the amount of time and effort this is taking. We still need the result, so I need to find an easier way of doing this."

Those two thoughts—getting great results with less work—are at the core of much great leadership!

I am not saying that you need to be selfish and self-centered in a nasty way to get ahead. But you do need to focus on yourself enough, to give yourself time to think and manage your energy. Then you can optimize your efforts instead of just working yourself to death and not getting anywhere.

Being Self-*Less* Isn't the Best Way to Help Others

Many people are very strongly driven to give to others. That is a good thing. But don't get caught up in thinking that the only way you can feel satisfied that you are giving to others is through suffering.

If putting yourself last feels virtuous, just know that you are missing an opportunity to excel and you are kidding yourself that you are doing it for others. Giving others every last drop of your energy *doesn't equate to maximizing what you can give others*. The better and stronger you are, the more you can give. It's a basic tenet in any survival situation; you know: "Put your own oxygen mask on first and then help others."

Great leaders and high performers know this. The right kind of productive selfishness and laziness motivates and allows you to take care of yourself so you are in an even better position to lead and help others.

Just Because You *Can* Work Tirelessly Doesn't Mean You *Should*

It can be really tempting to devote all your time and energy to working, particularly if you are ambitious and competing for a big promotion. But you need to break out of the mode of being overly busy, to give yourself a chance to do the things that are truly necessary to advance.

The easiest way to break the cycle is to have something really important competing for your time. In my case, as I was building my career I had the challenge of having some health issues. I won't bore you with the details, but suffice it to say, I felt that I had less physical energy than a normal person. I simply couldn't work 24/7. If I worked long days or traveled extensively, I needed to recover on the weekends. In hindsight, this was so lucky for me. I am sure that if I had had the energy to keep working, I would have filled the time with more work.

But here was my career issue. Even though I couldn't work as many extra hours as my peers, I still wanted to stand out and get ahead. So I was forced to find a way to do higher-value work in less time. In my case, that was not my brilliant strategic thinking, it was just my reality.

I now fully recognize that my "liability" was, in fact, really a stroke of luck. It enabled me to get it right. While many of my peers stayed overbusy, I was forced to find a way to work at a higher level of value. And my built-in regulator—periodically needing some rest—gave me an advantage of extra time to think.

It is not a requirement to have something specific pulling you away from working all the time, but it is a big help. Because if you have a lot of energy, and there's nothing competing for your time and nothing emotionally pulling you away from work—like family, hobbies, or community—you are more likely to stay overbusy.

If this sounds like you, be careful not to fall into the trap of thinking you are superior—that putting all of your extra time into work gives you an advantage. It doesn't. If you truly want to spend every waking hour working, make sure your extra work is adding value and moving something significant forward, not just filling time with more work. (You'd be much better off with a pet, a date, or a hobby!)

KEY INSIGHT: *You may fall into the trap where you fail to create real value because you have so much energy to just muscle through all the work!*

Here is an example of how this can backfire. I was talking to an executive at one of the big Silicon Valley tech companies. She was trying to teach her team this lesson: *you can't work yourself to death and succeed over the long term.* It was a hard cultural challenge, because her team believed that this overwork was not only highly valued by the company, but *demanded.*

Then, while they were working at this frantic, nonstop pace and delivering all this output, the company laid off half the team. It's a sad lesson: not only did the company *not* value all that extra work, but they decided that they didn't even need half of it! You need to pick where you are going to add value (DO Better) *and* make sure the company actually values it (LOOK Better). Then do it in a sustainable way so you can keep delivering important outcomes.

* * *

The Hard (and Important) Part

No one will ever give you permission to be less busy. It can feel scary to stop appearing really busy if you associate your value with the amount of time you spend working. Just know that it's not the *work* that matters; it's the *outcomes* you deliver. You don't win the game for running up and down the court; it's the points on the board that count.

Refuse to burn up all your time on things that are not so important. Trust that giving yourself time to think will help you find ways to deliver higher-value business outcomes and get the right work done in less time. People will see you delivering real value, getting smarter and faster—not just working really hard. It will get less scary.

Next . . . How to focus your work on the highest-value business outcomes

2. Ruthless Priorities

Overachieve Where It Counts

Here is one of the biggest executive "secrets" that is lived out in broad daylight.

Don't Do Everything

Once you make it a point to observe this, you will notice it everywhere. But it's not obvious if you are not looking for it.

Simply put, highly successful people don't do everything.

Watch them. They drop the ball on all kinds of things. They disappoint people. They may have disappointed *you* from time to time.

But if they are successful, the other thing that you will notice is that they have a ruthless focus on the things they care about. It may seem that they are not doing a good job—but maybe that is just on the part that you are looking at. You need to understand: what else are they doing?

What you are seeing is that they are not doing a *complete* job. And that's because they have mastered the art of not doing everything.

And what they *are* doing are those few things that will make the biggest impact on the business—and they are doing them very well.

KEY INSIGHT: *The ability to work this way is not a status that is granted to you. These people were not given permission to focus on a few things and drop others. They were not less busy or less constrained than others. They took risks. They worked it out. You need to work it out.*

Too Much Work

I spoke to a midlevel manager in a telecom company, a man who was very stressed about the workload being placed on his team. He told me that the executives didn't seem to notice or care that his team was maxed out.

He was very concerned because his team had been working over capacity for some time, and they were getting burned out. He didn't think even the current level of work was sustainable, but the execs kept piling the work on. He felt terrible about asking his team to take on even more.

To make matters worse, the organization had recently downsized, so he was getting additional work from other teams. They initially told him he could make some hires to fill some key positions, but now they were not allowing the hires.

And every time he tried to prioritize and stop doing something, someone got angry. They insisted that he must add it back or they would die, or they would go over his head to his boss. The worst part was, it was his boss who was adding the most work and being the most unreasonable.

I have this conversation over and over again with managers in all kinds of companies.

KEY INSIGHT: *Welcome to being a leader. This is your job. Your job is not to deliver work when everything lines up to support you. Your job is to get the most important stuff done* despite *everything that lines up to kill you.*

Your job is to deal with the overload and the lack of personal support and to negotiate room, keep your boss and stakeholders at bay, and keep your team on board.

This is indeed one of the hardest things leaders deal with and therefore one of the key things that sets the most successful leaders apart.

The most successful leaders are able to fend off the endless demands and get the critical stuff done, no matter who and what is trying to throw them off course.

Don't Just Accept Work—Redefine It

The way successful executives get away with not doing everything is by redefining the work as it comes in and negotiating a different, smaller, higher-value set of work.

KEY INSIGHT: *You need to* catch *all the work, but not* do *all the work.*

As a manager, you are expected to analyze all the tasks that come in, contain them, and propose a plan that will have the biggest impact on the business. You need to choose from all the work you are getting and map out the right work to achieve the right desired business outcomes.

KEY INSIGHT: *The work almost never comes across the table at you the way you should do it.*

It's a key part of your job to think through the overwhelming workload and to rework it. Yes, you need to deliver the results, but you don't necessarily need to do it by completing the ten assignments that come to you, as requested. What if combining three of them into one, dropping four, doing three as defined, and adding a new one is the best way to deliver the desired outcome? It's your job to realize that and propose it.

If you just try and do everything that is asked of you, you fail in two key ways:

1. You can't possibly do it all, so you will fail to deliver some things.

2. But more important, that's the wrong job anyway. If you don't apply strategic thinking and judgment to tune the workload, your boss doesn't need you. She could just as easily assign all the work directly to your team. Your job is to make sense of it and prioritize it correctly and show how a redefined workload delivers the necessary results. This adds real value—and lets you succeed.

Advise Your Executive

Here is the secret. Your boss *wants* you to push back. Your boss is expecting you to think through the business strategy and the workload and offer advice—not to just try and do everything. I know that what I wanted from my staff was for them to catch all the work, analyze it, make judgments about business priorities, and come back to me and negotiate. I wanted them to debate with me about what is most important and why and suggest how to rework the plan to do the most important things first. *Your boss needs you to help her with her thinking.* You are being paid to judge and decide, not to just do everything you are told.

Who Stands Out?

The people who would come back to me with a thoughtful proposal for what to do and in what order, that would be good for the business, and doable for the team, were the ones who stood out as high performers. The ones who didn't just accept all my ideas and requests, who *helped me think through* the strategy and priority stood out as high performers. The ones who tried to take on all the work and do everything, resulting in everything slipping, were not so impressive. The ones who simply ignored my inputs, kept their heads down, and did not step up to the strategic thinking and debate were not so impressive either.

Your Boss Forgets

There is a tendency to treat all requests from the boss equally. You need to resist this because they don't *intend them all equally.* They can seem equally excited or serious about a wide range of ideas; some are vitally important, others are just musings. It's hard to tell. They will often forget things that they asked for, or change their minds without telling you—you need to check.

Here's how to advise your executive and negotiate the workload:

- Keep a list of everything your boss asks for.

- Keep a list of the top strategic priorities you are working on.

- Have regular meetings with your boss where you take out these lists.

- Make recommendations about what to prioritize, based on the context of business and the content of these two lists.

When you show your boss these lists, several things happen:

- He gets embarrassed, as he hadn't realized he had asked for so many things. When he sees it spelled out right there in front of him, he can see it's unreasonable.

- You win lots of credibility for keeping the list, catching everything, and not dropping anything. You make him comfortable that you've got it covered. He trusts you.

- You can ask him "Is this still important?" You will find he has forgotten about several of the requests and has decided that others don't matter anymore.

- You will realize that you are not beholden to everything on the list!

- You will be able to negotiate time lines and suggest priorities.

Manage Risks

Ruthless Priorities are the result of this thinking, of mapping the work to high-value business outcomes. They are those few things that have a bigger impact on the business than anything else. No matter what, these must get done. Ruthless Priorities are those few things that you refuse to put at risk.

This doesn't mean that all the other stuff isn't important, too. That's why you have to be ruthless. Being ruthless elevates the truly critical stuff above the really important stuff.

This implies, of course, that for everything else, you will tolerate some risk. It doesn't mean that you completely drop everything else; it means that you are willing to put everything else at some level of risk to make sure that your Ruthless Priorities are not put at risk at all.

You can consider taking longer to do them or doing them at a lower level of quality or completeness. That's OK, because you are going to do a remarkable job on the things that count more—your Ruthless Priorities.

Your Success Rides on This

KEY INSIGHT: *Because you are genuinely succeeding at the things that have the biggest impact on this business, you'll be forgiven for the things you don't get done.*

For example, I know a chief operating officer (COO) of a retail company who intentionally dropped the ball on many tactical, high-priority infrastructure projects to make sure that the most strategic things were on track. For almost a year, he put all his focus on rolling out, nationwide, a new point-of-sale system that would help the business run new loyalty-based sales promotions. This was going to drive increased revenue to the business. He delayed a large backlog of demands and projects, because he realized this new system would have a much bigger impact on the business than all the other things combined.

He understood the business. He took the risk. He said "no" a lot. Although people were annoyed that he was late on those other things, he was forgiven. He was able to succeed on a key project that opened up a new revenue stream for the business. He created success where it really counted because he gave himself enough bandwidth to do a great job on the most important thing first.

Do the Math

If you try to do a hundred things and spread your energy among them, you will never do as good a job at any one thing as will those who are applying two-thirds of their time and energy to just three things. If you try to do everything on your plate to an equal level of quality, you will not give yourself the chance to excel where it matters.

Let's face it. You are not going to get everything on your list done anyway.

So instead of failing to do 30 percent of it, fail to do 40 percent of it on purpose and give yourself the ability to score a huge win on something that has a really big impact on the business.

I don't want to imply that this is easy or obvious. The choices you need to make to support Ruthless Priorities are painful, but it's more painful not to excel at *anything* because you try to do *everything*.

10 Steps to Ruthless Priorities

1. Identify what matters most to the business.

2. Choose your Ruthless Priorities.

3. Focus on what you *are* doing, not on what you are *not* doing.

4. Ratify your Ruthless Priorities with your boss.

5. Assign less than 100 percent of your time.

6. Resist or negotiate away pressures that put Priorities at risk.

7. Overcommunicate.

8. Create a new social norm.

9. Get them done. Finish things!

10. Recognize and celebrate.

Let's look at each of these in detail.

1. Identify What Matters Most to the Business

Ruthless Priorities always start with the business objectives. You need to educate yourself on what the business values. Whatever is happening in your functional area must be considered in the context of what is most important to the business overall. Make sure you know how the business makes money, grows, and is being measured.

Get really clear about what is most important to the business right now. Is it revenue growth, profit growth, geographic expansion, operational efficiency, customer care, product quality, competitiveness, or sales channel evolution?

KEY INSIGHT: *You need to get really clear about how all the activity in your team or function truly impacts the business (or doesn't). You need to connect the dots between your workload and the most important and significant business outcomes.*

I remember a time when a product team in a commercial building-supply company was running around to the point of chaos, trying to react to competitive pressures in the market. They were being told by the sales force that they were losing deals based on not having competitive products. They were trying to respond to every sales situation where the company was competing and losing.

Finally, a program manager on the team stepped back and did a more thorough analysis of what was happening in these deals. She realized that the product issues were not the primary reason they were losing business. They had a very serious channel conflict issue. Basically, their dealers were promoting the competitor's product much more aggressively because they made more money on them. The company had a bad agreement with a big distributor who was undercutting the rest of their dealers.

With this information about what was really impacting the business, she got the sales organization focused on fixing the channel issue and got the product team back to developing a much more innovative product line. Once they stopped trying to respond to everything, they were able to build a highly competitive product.

Being really clear about the business impact of your work is the context and the backdrop for adding more value. This is also the specific test to use to evaluate, choose, and negotiate your Ruthless Priorities.

2. Choose Your Ruthless Priorities

In the beginning, before you go through this exercise, it always seems like *everything* is really important. Nothing ever offers itself as a lower priority.

Here is an example. A marketing organization is facing a quarter in which they need to support a launch, a sales meeting, an analyst meeting, and an acquisition. There is way too much work to go around. The temptation is to say, "These are all really important" and try to work on all of them with an equal level of commitment.

But if you've gone through step #1, you can step back and consider the overall business situation, market climate, sales momentum, competitive moves, and Wall Street expectations.

The company may have a tragic and controversial corporate story at the moment, so this may be the analyst meeting of all time. Failure to excel with Wall Street will put the final nail in the coffin. In that case, you don't drop the other three, but you support the analyst meeting first and foremost until it is done to an exceptional level of preparation and quality.

Alternatively, if the business is in a turnaround situation and the sales force has not been selling, you realize that if you fail to motivate and train the sales force, you will have no sales channel. That becomes a Ruthless Priority. It would be a bad decision not to overachieve on that. So you need to make sure you give yourself the bandwidth to create the best sales event ever. In that case you tell the analysts that you are making a huge investment in the sales channel, and they will get more details later. You tune the launch deliverables to support the sales force, with customer references and lead generation. And you decide to do less rigorous PR initially and delay local launch events until the next quarter—right now it's all about sales tools and relationships.

Here's a trick: If you only think about why things are important, you will always be stuck thinking everything is important. Try another approach. Ask your team, "How bad is it if we fail?" You will then see an actual priority emerge.

If you really understand the business climate, you can ask yourself and your team about each of the competing priorities: what happens if we fail? The answer will differ depending on the business situation, but going through this thought process about what actually happens and how bad it would be if you fail will help point you to the Ruthless Priorities.

I often use the actual phrase "Can't Fails" when selecting Ruthless Priorities, because it implies a "butt-on-the-line" kind of accountability and seriousness. I find it helps expose all the really important things that, if we fail at them, won't *kill us*. It makes the Can't Fails stand out loud and clear.

Here's another example: In a software company I worked at, we had two serious problems with our product. Our product features were uncompetitive, and we also had significant quality problems. We chose. Instead of trying to improve quality to improve customer satisfaction *and* add features to address competitiveness, we focused an entire development cycle on just fixing bugs and quality issues.

The competition edged ahead in the short term, but ultimately we created a much higher-quality base to add new features to later, and we were able to win back customers through our quality initiative. Quality became the Can't Fail because we realized that we would lose more customers with poor quality than we would gain with new features in the short term. We would lose current customers who got fed up with us, we would not have good references to convert new prospects into customers, and our product trials and demos would not provide a positive enough experience to get people to buy. If we had lost current customers and failed to win new customers, the business would have failed.

More important, if we had tried to do both quality and features, we would have done neither well in the time frame of the release. By choosing one that we would not put at risk and delaying the other one, we achieved a solid success on the one we permitted ourselves to focus on. And we put ourselves in a position to compete better over the long term.

You have to choose. Select one to three (no more than five) initiatives or tasks that support what matters most to the business. These are your Ruthless Priorities.

KEY INSIGHT: *It's not that you can choose the important things over things that are not important. The ruthless part comes in when you prioritize the vitally important Can't Fails over other really important things.*

3. Focus on What You *Are* Doing, Not on What You Are *Not* Doing

You wouldn't suddenly announce to the world, "These are all the things I am *not* doing." That's not going to impress anyone.

The more you can focus on the importance of what you *are* doing and its strategic value to the business, the more support and understanding you will get when people don't see equally great performance from you on everything else. So you use your Ruthless Priorities to demonstrate that you have identified and are executing on the most critical things, and you take the position of making it clear that you will not put these things at risk and that you will focus on them until they are complete.

You may need to give people a heads-up that some other items that are not on this list may not be achieved as soon as expected, but if you have sold them on the value of what you *are* doing and showed them its critical impact on the business, they will not be able to argue with you (and if they try, they will not win).

4. Ratify Your Ruthless Priorities with Your Boss

You don't want your boss to be caught off-guard about something you have chosen not to do, or not to do as well. But again, you don't want to go to your boss and announce all the things you are not doing. That won't work.

You need to go to your boss and sell him on the idea of why it is so important that the *top* few things you have identified can't fail. You need to get him as committed as you are to deliver on these few things. You need to inspire him with your plan to overachieve on them and why it matters. Once you do that, you can show him the rest of the list and get his agreement to support you if those less-critical things get done more slowly or at a lower level of excellence.

This is how you keep your boss from continuing to pile things on. Get him on the hook for the same critical business outcomes—your Ruthless Priorities.

When I drove this conversation with my bosses, one of three things typically happened:

1. My boss not only agreed, but focused even more on key outcomes and took more off my plate. (This is the best response, but requires a good sales job on your part as well as a smart boss.)

2. My boss was not thinking as strategically as I was but welcomed my pushing him to think through the business impacts and ultimately agreed to pare down the list of tasks.

3. My boss didn't support my way of thinking and pushed back.

What If Your Boss Doesn't Agree with Your Ruthless Priorities?

The reality is, you can't win against your boss. You need to either negotiate or concede.

But you also can't blame your failure on the fact that your boss is stupid. You need to find a way to create successful outcomes even when your boss isn't helping.

If your boss is not agreeing with your Ruthless Priorities, you have two choices.

1. **Enlighten your boss.** Your boss may be very stuck in the details. Try again. If you show your boss how some things are a bigger priority than others because they impact the business more, you can sometimes get that lightbulb to go on. Then you can get support for your Ruthless Priorities.

2. **Accept your boss's opinion.** If your boss simply disagrees that the Ruthless Priorities you have selected are the most important things, then understand what his views are and take his direction on what your Ruthless Priorities are. The last thing you need to waste time on is driving Ruthless Priorities that your boss doesn't care about.

Yes, you need to find a way to succeed if your boss is being stupid, but if your plan requires you to win against your boss, you will lose, even if you are right. One way or another, get your Ruthless Priorities aligned and ratified with your boss.

If your boss refuses to take anything off your plate, you need to go back with a priority and say, "I am going to finish this first." Then do the next thing.

Don't let your boss try and push you into working on everything at the same time. You will fail.

5. Assign Less Than 100 Percent of Your Time

Things happen. There will always be urgent emergencies that you have to deal with. You need to be realistic about how much time this takes in your world and keep some unassigned time to deal with it. Otherwise you are putting your Ruthless Priorities at risk from the get-go. This is exactly what you are setting out to *not* do.

6. Resist or Negotiate Away Pressures That Put Priorities at Risk

You will get internal and external pressure to change course. Resist it.

There will always be reasons for people to question whether your Ruthless Priorities are still important. New things will come up. People will argue with you. There will be squeaky wheels whose pet projects are not being focused on. There will be pressure from the sales force and other organizations. Your boss will forget what she agreed to.

The more you use the following answer—"We will fit that in as long as it does not put our Ruthless Priorities at risk"—the more you will be able to avoid distraction and keep your organization on course to deliver.

You need to stay on course, because if you don't, you will just go back to lots of activity and not doing a great job at anything in particular. And you will have lost ground on all the other most important things.

> **KEY INSIGHT:** *You can get away with not achieving everything if you deliver remarkable results on the few key things. But if you don't actually achieve your Ruthless Priorities, you then have no success to offset why you didn't do better at everything else.*

Don't lose your nerve. Stick to it. If you're tempted to work on everything because it feels less risky, just realize that you will remain unremarkable because you have not given yourself the opportunity to really excel on something that has a big impact on the business.

7. Overcommunicate

You need to communicate your Ruthless Priorities over and over and over again. Say them in an all-hands meeting every week or month. List them in your email signature. Start and finish every one-on-one meeting with them. Unless you are completely sick and tired of talking about your message, you aren't even close to getting your audience to adopt it.

I know a manager who was a master at this. He would pick one Ruthless Priority for the year, and he would pretty much refuse to talk about anything else. He knew that other stuff was being worked on too, but in terms of what he was willing to spend time talking about, at any point in time, it was just one thing.

You need to let people know you are serious. You cannot possibly overcommunicate your Ruthless Priorities.

Use the 21-Times Rule

There is a well-tested marketing principle that says that for your audience to understand your message well enough to act on it, they must hear or see your message seven times. And for every one time they consciously see it or hear it, they have to be exposed to it three times, thus, the "21-Times Rule."

I can tell you without question or hesitation, twenty-one times is not overkill.

Earlier in this chapter, I mentioned a software company I worked for, where we chose quality over features as our Ruthless Priority over a six-month period. This was a very simple message: "Improve quality. For six months we will only fix bugs. No new features will be added." Every Friday afternoon we had an all-hands meeting. And in each and every one we would reiterate this message. And for seventeen weeks in a row, someone always asked the question, "But shouldn't we be putting new features in?"

Really: twenty-one times is a minimum.

Be unfailingly consistent. Only when you are mind-numbingly bored with talking about your Ruthless Priorities will your organization really know you are serious and feel confident about acting on them.

8. Create a New Social Norm

The gravitational pull of going back to the old way is really strong.

Making the progress on a Ruthless Priority part of the social fabric of your organization is critical. Getting people at all levels talking about it provides an additional confidence boost, beyond just your communicating. Get your people talking to you and each other about what is expected and how it is going. How are they doing? What is working? What is challenging?

> **KEY INSIGHT:** *If you have not made your team feel comfortable that staying focused on the Ruthless Priority is the right thing to do, when an urgent customer deal or sales request comes in, some people will automatically jump back into reactive mode.*

And then the people who are trying to stay focused on the Ruthless Priority, when they see a colleague being reactive, will pause. Without seeing any social signs within the team that others are still committed to the new behavior, they will think that the rules have changed back to the status quo.

Live the Dream

Here is a great example of how conversational, social review of progress with the whole team helps lock in desired behaviors.

I worked with a team in a media consulting business. They had a Ruthless Priority of generating higher-value client engagements. But that meant carving time out of their current way of working to do a new, more strategic kind of outreach.

They agreed that they would each spend one hour per day specifically on developing this new business. In this hour, they planned to reach out to their networks of current clients. The goal was to get leads, introductions, and referrals for their new, more strategic engagements.

It worked for a couple of days. People were using an hour each day to make the calls. But after a couple of days, the standard tactical pressures and urgent demands kicked back in. Clients were requesting things, email kept coming in, and the phones kept ringing. Some people got sucked right back into the reactive stuff.

Because the team did not talk regularly about the new way of working, because they did not share their progress and struggles with each other, they lost focus and confidence. The people who were still carving out the hour to do the strategic outreach started getting nervous. They saw the rest of the team working in the old way. This made it seem like the urgent stuff really *was* more important, because they hadn't heard about the new stuff lately.

I see this happen all the time. People won't know that you are serious about getting your Ruthless Priority done if you don't make it part of the social fabric of your team.

The solution: They decided that every day at 2 p.m. they would gather as a team for five minutes and ask the question: "Who has done their hour of strategic outreach today? How did it go?" By talking about it every single day as a group, they kept the new idea alive and in focus in their work day. It remained clear to everyone that this was still important—this was still the right thing to be doing. Simply by talking about the new expectation as a group, people felt more accountable and more comfortable doing it.

And they did it! They achieved their desired outcome of bringing in more, higher-value business.

9. Get Them Done

Most people just want to make progress—on something. Organizations that are stretched too thin and trying to do too many things are just not fun to work in. People like to finish things. Getting things done motivates your team and your customers and buys you goodwill and confidence from both groups.

Also, if you are known for delivering, you have a lot of power. You will have built-in support when things don't go exactly according to plan.

They will trust that you will finish what you say you are doing and then be able to get the next thing done. This is having real power in an organization.

10. Recognize and Celebrate

Give credit where credit is due and shine a spotlight on your team's success. Use this as an opportunity to reinforce your model of sticking to your Ruthless Priorities. Take the opportunity to promote the fact that this is the way you lead and that it works.

The other side of the coin here is that it is important not to reward and celebrate heroics that do *not* support the Ruthless Priority. You're always going to have those who disagree and go off and do something different, but you can avoid praising them for it.

A good example happened at a product development organization that I did some consulting for. The Ruthless Priority was to increase predictability of delivering, and the team had committed to implement a new process to keep things on track.

A sales rep made a direct call to a developer who then went outside the process and built something as a one-off for that sales rep. The sales rep won the deal.

However, that maneuver on the part of the developer caused a delay in the overall program. That delay had a cost. The credibility of the organization took a huge hit, and the deal cost the company more business in the long term than that one deal had brought in. The division manager wisely did not celebrate the small win, because it went against the larger process and the Ruthless Priority.

Pick the Next Three and Repeat

You don't always even have to pick the exact right things. Getting big things done is so powerful that you will get smarter as you do it. Getting things done helps you see around corners. You learn, because you can actually test the reality of the impact of what you got done. If it succeeds, great! If it doesn't, learn, adjust, and get the next thing done.

You can pick the next three priorities, and people will trust you to deliver again. Your team will be motivated because they know you won't jerk them around and change the rules. They will begin to help you stick to the priorities because they like what it feels like to deliver, and they like to see how what they do is connected to moving the business forward.

* * *

The Hard (and Important) Part

Identifying and sticking to Ruthless Priorities is one of the hardest things you need to do. Not only is no one giving you permission to focus, but people—maybe even your boss—are mostly fighting against you.

But you must focus. If you don't, you will work very hard but fail to deliver significant business outcomes. So you will fail. This is one of those lonely leadership moments. All leaders face this. The most successful ones get on top of it. They rise above the work.

It's critical to recognize that your job as a leader is to collect and respond to all of the requests that come from above, but *not* to try to actually *do* them all. You are expected to tune the workload, to change the game, to figure out better ways to do things. You need to show your executive management why some things are more important than others, and then to deliver on the right ones.

If your executive management could figure out which of the things, in all of this work they assign to you, were truly critical to the business, they wouldn't need you. That's your job.

KEY INSIGHT: *Think of your job more as figuring out a better way to deal with all this stuff than it is to DO all this stuff and you'll be on the right track.*

Trying to do everything may avoid some conflict and arguments in the short term but sets you up for failure in the long term. And nothing will ever offer itself up as a lower priority. You need to figure it out. You need to distinguish and elevate the critical few Can't Fails from all the other very important stuff on the plate.

Prioritize, negotiate through the conflict, stick to your guns, and get the most important stuff done. You're not going to get any credit for working hard on everything if you fail to get the critical things done well. If you must be known for working hard, be known for working hard on things that really matter and for keeping those on course amid distractions.

Next . . . Now that you are focused on what's important, make even more time to do it.

3. Make More Time

Successful People Make More Time

Even when you are focused on Ruthless Priorities, there is still never enough time in the day. And it is very likely that the things keeping you most busy are annoying time wasters and fire drills—not your Ruthless Priorities.

So when you are out of time, you need to make more. Think about it this way: If you had 20 percent more time magically appear in your work week—a full uncommitted, unscheduled work day, every week—what would you do with it?

Would you do more email? Would you go to more bad meetings? Would you do even more of what you are already doing? Or would you do something different—and better?

There will always be times when a crisis or opportunity emerges, and you need to work what feels like 24/7 for some period of time to accomplish something critical or extraordinary. That is reality. But that needs to be the exception. If you work that way all the time, you need to make a change to get yourself out of that mode if you want to grow your success.

Schedule Time and *Hide*

Take some time back. Just take it. Actually schedule time to think. If you have no time to think, you will continue to use up all your time.

For a start, schedule two hours per week and *hide*. The world will not come to an end. The hiding part is important. Otherwise, this doesn't work—the activity knows where to find you.

This time is just for you—to think, to plan, to focus on what's most critical, reprioritize, delegate, and create processes. You will never be able to even list your Ruthless Priorities if you don't give yourself time to think. Remember: You are not taking two hours away from getting work done. You are investing two hours in getting more of the right things done, better.

If you do this, you will find that you free up even more time. For example, if you take two hours to improve a process or clarify an outcome or delegate a task, you could gain another five hours in saved time. Then you use those five hours to communicate more effectively and reassess priorities and outcomes for your team. When those efforts then take hold, you have created even more time, and so on. . . .

It is a core trait of the most successful people to rise above being overbusy. If there are any secrets to what really successful people do, this is one of them. They make more time.

Here are some more strategies you can think about to make more time.

Make the Container Smaller

It's like the ideal gas law: A gas will expand to fill the size of its container, no matter how big the container. Likewise, the amount of activity in any job will always expand to fill your time, no matter what the job and no matter how much time you allow.

It's up to you to contain it—make your container of time for your current activities smaller. Once you do that, you will be forced to make it fit. For example, what would happen if you limited doing email to one hour per day? Would the world end? Or would you learn to deal with the most important stuff first? Decide how much time various areas of work are worth, and don't exceed that amount of time.

Seek and Destroy Chaos

Let's face it: there are huge amounts of chaos in organizations. And we are all our own personal chaos generators, too.

People always complain about being overbusy and stretched too thin, but, surprisingly, they don't do some of the basic things they could do to make more time.

Stop chaos. Prevent chaos. Wake up every morning with the intent of finding and eliminating some chaos.

For Starters, Deal with Your Task List and Email

There are lots of time management tools out there. Use them; you need them. Think about how much time you spend looking for lost emails, juggling multiple to-do lists, and searching for the components of what you are working on. Just fix this stuff. You will add several hours of new productive time to your week.

Fix Poor Communication

Poor communication in organizations is another time sink. When communications are not clear, the number of questions and individual conversations rises exponentially. Be really clear about decisions, priorities, and issues, and find a communication mechanism to distribute the information. You will increase the capacity of your team greatly if you simply communicate better.

I know that as a leader I would often send an email to a group that was locked in a festering "reply to all" argument. Mine would read as follows: "This is the LAST EMAIL on this topic. All of you please meet on this and bring me your decision by the end of the day, or I will make the decision myself. But no more email on this."

Fix Bad Meetings

I don't tolerate people being late to meetings. It is a huge waste of time. I don't tolerate meetings without a clearly defined desired outcome. I don't tolerate meetings where the necessary people are not in the room to accomplish the outcome. I don't tolerate email in meetings.

Most people accept the fact that people will be late to meetings. You all sit there and people come and go for ten or fifteen minutes. You start the meeting without everyone there, and then you need to recover the ground when they come in.

Don't live this way. The most effective people don't. It doesn't take long to develop a new habit. You need to show people you are serious, and make very sure you start and end on time. Try having 25- and 50-minute meetings instead of 30- and 60-minute meetings. Give people a chance to not be late and then call them on it if they are. Improving your meeting behaviors can add hours to everyone's week.

I often get asked, "But how do you get people to be on time for meetings and what do you do when they are not? You can't really fire them for being late to a meeting, can you?" I think people make this harder than it needs to be. You have to call people out on being late only a couple of times to get everyone to change their behavior. You need to be willing to live through some conflict to do it, but it is not a complicated process.

I learned this from a manager at a commercial real estate development company. He would simply say, "It's 8:04. What part of 'This meeting starts at 8 a.m.' did you not understand? When I say the meeting starts at 8:00, I expect you to be here and ready to start at 8:00."

Believe me, everyone in the room feels uncomfortable at this point, and they don't want to be the person this happens to next time. You really need to do this only once or twice and then people will be on time!

Be Selectively Responsive

We live in an "always on" world. We are global employees. Twenty-four hours a day, someone is working and asking you for something. The trick is to be seen as responsive without actually responding to everything! This is another reason why it is so important to have your Ruthless Priorities clearly defined and publicized. You need to be very responsive on matters relating to your Ruthless Priorities—but you can let some other things go.

Don't get hung up on responding fully to everything that comes your way. It will kill you. Sometimes a short "Got it" email is all you ever need to do. You get points for being responsive, but you don't really spend time on it.

I know a customer advocate in a consulting company. She gets so much email, she doesn't even try to read it. She just files it all in folders arranged by sender. Most of it, she never needs to touch again. When something is important and her phone rings, she simply searches for the right folder, retrieves the referenced email, and deals with it in the moment. Which is a good lead-in to the next point. . . .

Leave Some Things Unresolved

This is one of the biggest sources of making time that many people often miss. Don't resolve things that don't need to be resolved.

If you are good at fixing things or just can't stand unanswered questions, open loops, or disorganize data, get over it. You can't fix everything, and most of it doesn't matter anyway. Go back to your Ruthless Priorities. If your unresolved issues have nothing to do with executing on your most critical business initiatives, leave them unresolved.

We all have our own psychological needs and drivers that tempt us into wasting time on digging into unresolved issues. For me, I was always embarrassed when something in my organization was being done stupidly. I had to get over it. I realized that although fixing it might offer an efficiency improvement in one area, it would take me away from what I really needed to be doing. It would have made me feel better but because it did not serve my Ruthless Priorities, it was bad for the business.

A finance manager in a big company told me, "We waste huge amounts of time being 100 percent accurate when it doesn't matter." If you are providing decision support to a business leader and can determine that the cost of project will be $12,000,000, it is not worth spending an extra two weeks reconciling the past expenses to determine that it will likely cost $12,000,147.

What is your hook? Do you need things to be organized perfectly? Do you need to fix things? Do you need to solve puzzles? Do you need to resolve disputes? Identify your psychological trap, face it head on, and learn to leave things unresolved.

You will save whole days.

Have a "Don't Do" List

This is a technique a colleague of mine uses when she is super busy and does not want to put her key results at risk. She makes a *Don't Do* list, which notes the things she will be tempted to spend time on: internet browsing, organizing old data, studying issues of interest. On this list she also put her list of nagging business issues to leave unresolved for the time being. It's a good tool to remind yourself of the lower-value things that could use up your time and are most likely to tempt you away from your hard, important work.

Deal with Feeling Overwhelmed

In my experience, the worst thing about being overwhelmed is *feeling* overwhelmed.

Being overwhelmed is actually not that bad. We all have experienced successfully navigating overwhelming demands. The big issue is the stress that comes from worrying about everything you are supposed to be doing and the concern that you are going to drop something important, disappoint someone, or miss a critical commitment.

Thinking about all the things you need to do can snowball into what feels like an uncontrollable avalanche of responsibilities. And you tend to get locked into a repeating loop of thinking about it all. It's hugely stressful facing the same thoughts, decisions, and issues over and over again and not resolving them.

Really do this. This is a process I started to use fifteen years ago to deal with an overwhelming work load, and it works so well I have done it ever since.

Make three lists on one sheet of paper, in three columns.

In the first column, list the things on your to-do list that you are actually getting done.

In the second column, list things that you have committed to get done to your boss or your customers or your peers or your team—but are not getting done.

In the third column, list the things that you know are really important, but that you have no chance in hell of being able to do because of the existence of the first two lists.

Things I am getting done	Things you think I am doing that I am not	Things I know are important that I can't get to at all

Here is where the magic of this chart happens. . . .

First, I find the act of just getting it all down on paper and out of your head reduces the stress levels significantly. For one, seeing it all in one place gives you a feeling of control and absolves you of the thought attack—incessantly creating pieces of the list over and over again in your head.

Second, it's the middle list that is the source of most of the stress: things you have committed to someone—your boss, your team, your peers, your family—that you will be doing, but you're not. This is the one that feels really bad and wakes you up at 3 a.m. This list of things you are on the hook for but are not getting done is the source of the feeling of being overwhelmed. This list is never as long as it feels. So when you get it down on paper and see that it is only twelve things, not thirty-five, you feel much better.

Remember, this is not just about work. You will have a work-only version of this to share with your boss and team, but it's good to do another version for yourself that has the additional commitments you have made to your family or others outside of work. All these things are competing for your time and mental bandwidth, so it's important for you to get it all down in one place and assess it.

Finally, it gives you a proactive way to renegotiate your workload with yourself, your boss, and your team (and your family).

Once you have these lists, you can judge whether the right things are in the right columns. You can use the lists to have a discussion with your manager. You will be able to negotiate moving things among the three lists and dropping some things entirely. You will often find that you are stressing out about things your manager no longer really cares about.

I know a woman in a publishing company who uses this chart and refers to it as her "honest pass." It allows her to talk to her boss and her peers in a straightforward and safe way. She then can get everyone on the same page about her Ruthless Priorities and what they will agree to wait for.

This is also a gift you can give to your team. Ask them to go through this process and then help them reprioritize their work load. Encourage them to share these lists with each other. When they see each others' lists, they will often begin to trade and share work. You can experience an almost automatic optimization of the workload across your team.

For more help with making time, see "Working the Right Way" in the Resources section on page 267.

Build Your Energy

It's important to note that the people who are getting ahead are not the ones who are burned out, used up, and pissed off. Most of them are kind of OK.

KEY INSIGHT: *Highly successful people manage their energy on purpose. It's hard to overstate the importance of managing energy.*

Having more energy multiplies your time. You don't just work faster; you take on things you wouldn't otherwise. You solve bigger problems and pursue bigger challenges. You have more to give to others. You help your team and your peers more. You have more confidence and make better decisions.

Maximizing your energy is not optional. If you want to succeed as a leader, you need to drive big, creative outcomes in the business. You simply can't do this with low energy. So it's very important to understand what gives you energy and what drains it, and to have a plan to do more of the energy-building stuff and less of the energy-draining stuff on purpose.

Here are just a few ways to build up your energy.

Don't Squander Your Prime Time

Know when you are at your best. Consider the time of day and the days of the week when you are at your peak, energy-wise. When is it that you can think most clearly and are most motivated? Is it first thing in the morning, late at night, cocktail hour, Saturday morning? Once you identify the time slot when you are the most focused and brilliant, for heaven's sake, don't spend it doing email! Don't go to bad meetings! Schedule that time for yourself and get your most important thinking and your most tough, creative, strategic, highest-value work done.

I have a brilliant colleague who is a very successful business leader. She describes her prime time, when she really needs to do tough, strategic work, as a quiet weekend alone with wine and a bag of cookies!

Be Fit

There is no single thing that can affect your energy more than being fit. If you think you have no time to exercise, think again. If you travel a lot, have a long commute, and are driving your children everywhere, you just need to work a little harder at planning.

A woman I know, who was working as marketing director of a national office supply chain, joined a cruddy gym across the street from where her son's hockey practice took place, so she got to work out a few times a week when she drove her son to hockey.

A man with a more than full-time job at a media company and a ridiculous commute focused his exercise on the weekends. He negotiated the time with his family to make sure his workouts fit into their weekend. And he negotiated with his manager to come in later one day a week so he could get another workout in the morning. His manager said to him, "Wow, I've always considered you to be someone with a huge amount of energy. I can't wait to see what you bring to the business if you have even more!"

Fitting in fitness is not impossible if you make it one of your personal Ruthless Priorities. You just refuse to put it at risk. Then you make it happen. Other things will move around it.

Be Generous

Generosity is a multiplier of energy. Help others. Have a sense of humor. Be grateful.

Don't stay angry. It takes a lot of energy to stay angry. The chemical response for anger lasts for one minute in your system. After that it is entirely your choice to stay angry. So to stay angry after one minute takes a lot of energy.

You will have disappointments in your career; get over them quickly. You will deal with jerks, and they will be offensive; ignore them and keep moving forward.

For example, I believe that a significant factor in my own personal success was being able to not react to the situations when I was treated unfairly because I was a woman. Looking back, I can certainly point to pay discrepancies, not getting considered for promotions, and lots of offensive and stupid behaviors along the way from managers and peers.

I genuinely believe that if I had made a big deal out of this and sought retribution because I was being mistreated as a woman—if I stayed angry, or focused my energy on this "not being fair"—it would have taken away from the energy I used to keep moving forward, delivering top results, and standing out in a positive way.

Don't Begrudge Others' Successes

Never begrudge other people their success. There will always be people who are ahead of you who you think don't deserve it. You may be tempted to begrudge them their success either because of their lack of capabilities or excellence or some unacceptable way that you think they got there in the first place.

This is completely wasted energy. Don't bother. Instead, learn something from it. Learn why and how they got there and then make your own decision whether that is something you would be willing to do. If not, get over it. There is absolutely no upside to crying "foul" instead of learning and moving forward.

Fail and Try Again

Successful people fail more than unsuccessful people.

They try a lot, they do a lot, and they fail a lot. They just get over it and keep going. Less successful people often play it safe or don't even try. Or when they fail, they get discouraged and just stop—game over.

Do stuff, fail, learn, and try again. Multiple times. See it instead as a step to your future success, and feel good that you are taking action. I don't know any highly successful people who have never been fired. Successful people can all name at least a few failures in their work and life. They are so successful because they tried again. Don't let failure drain your energy long term.

I love this quote by Mary Ann Radmacher:

> *Courage does not always roar. Sometimes courage is the quiet voice at the end of the day saying, "I will try again tomorrow."*

Deal with Slumps

As a human, you will go through periods in which you have low energy, you are discouraged, and you are not having fun—times when you get off your stride for a few weeks or months.

> **KEY INSIGHT:** *Don't assess your life or yourself when you are in a bad mood! There is no upside and no useful information will come of it. You are not [lazy, stupid, ineffective, unlikable, unattractive, slow, incompetent—wherever your mind goes]. You are in a slump. Wait till you are in a better mood—you'll get a better and more accurate assessment.*

Do things on purpose that help you recover your energy, but don't give yourself too hard a time for being in a slump along the way. If you keep moving forward in your life and your work, even if you are not at your most brilliant, the slump will eventually pass.

You work hard and you get tired. Sorry, but you are a human. The most successful people deal with slumps. The trick is not to let your head make them worse than they are.

Take Care of Yourself

Remember, you are being paid to think, to lead, to inspire others, to build relationships, to engage supporters, to motivate people, and to debate and negotiate and solve problems. Maintaining your energy is a personal Ruthless Priority for successful people.

If you are tired and stressed, you will not be doing your job as well, nor recognizing and creating opportunities that will set you apart. If your job is sapping your energy, you need to take some control back, get more sleep, get more exercise, get more renewal time. You are not doing your company any favors or impressing anyone with your stoic effort or your deteriorating health presented as proof of your undying personal commitment to your job. You are simply operating at a low capacity, and it's not good for anyone.

* * *

The Hard (and Important) Part

Urgent business demands will always come up. The pressure to schedule more than the time that you carved out for yourself will be strong. Your time will feel less important in the moment. You will feel guilty trying to reserve the time you need to think and build your energy.

Sometimes you will need to work around the clock and give up this time, but make sure that it is for special situations: crises, emergencies, big deals, and so on. In the general course of business, you must claim time for yourself. The world will not come to an end if you are not available for two hours a week. Just take it.

Next . . . How to put yourself in a position to thrive

4. The Agony and the Paycheck

Like Your Job More and Be Better at It

Once when flying across some vast expanse watching an especially beautiful sunset, the owner of the private plane stood behind the pilots, and said: "Is this what I pay you for, to sit back and relax in this $50 million jet watching the sun set?" to which the grizzled captain said, "No, you pay us to deal with all your bags, change your hotels, fix screwed-up rental car reservations, deal with catering mix-ups, get the airplane fixed, vacuum all the dog hairs up, and crap like that. This part we do for free."

Once you realize that your job is both your job description and dealing with all the crap that gets in the way of your doing your job description, and that what you are actually getting paid for is dealing with the crap, not the enjoyable parts, it all makes more sense.

Oops, the Crap *Is* the Job!

So many people land in the middle of their careers hating their jobs.

Or, if not actually hating it, feeling unsatisfied and thinking "What should I really be doing?" or "I am only doing this for the money, for just enough time until I'll have enough money so that I can *stop* doing this!"

"Do What You Love" Is Bad Advice

We all get told at some point (if not over and over again), "Do what you love and the money will follow," and it's just plain bad advice. The number of people who make a lot of money doing what they love is so insignificantly small that it's an unrealistic and useless thing to model. The most unfortunate thing about this is that it *makes people feel like they are failing when they don't achieve it.*

This plays out in two destructive ways:

1. Because they don't have the same feeling of love for their work that they do for their family or leisure activities, they feel like they are selling out or living life wrong. They waste a lot of time feeling unfulfilled, unhappy, or plagued by the feeling that they should be doing something different.

2. Others, who try to do the things they love full time, find that the effort to make a business of it and a living at it takes away all the enjoyment of it. They end up turning their love into a job they don't like, one that generally doesn't pay very well. They end up not loving life after all. And they waste time that they could have spent earning money.

Don't put this pressure on yourself!

KEY INSIGHT: *Consider thinking about your work/life strategy like this:*
-   *Do what you love for free.*
-   *Work for money.*
-   *Change how you do your job to feel less tortured about it—and maybe even feel pretty good about it.*

■ *Spend the money you make on doing the things you love when you're not at work.*

End of insight: Please read it again.

Oops, I Hate My Job—Now What?

I am not proposing that you sell your soul to a job you hate just to make a lot of money. I do believe, however, that you can make good money at a job that you don't love as much as you love your leisure activities, and that you are better off doing so.

During the middle of my career, when I was not enjoying my work, I was still wondering "What should I really be doing?" All the stories about people who gave up high-paying jobs they didn't like, took big financial cuts or risks to pursue their dreams, and were now so happy with their smaller, simpler, less expensive lives didn't help me. I wanted to stay in my comfortable home, buy nice shoes, drink good wine, *and* feel successful, happier, and more satisfied.

I felt stuck.

The problem was that I was in a technology career and I pretty much hated technology. My non–love affair with my work started in my first job out of college as an engineer in the Robotics Research Lab at Bell Labs, supporting the PhD researchers who were working to make robots respond intelligently to their environments. It would have been a dream job for some people, but I hated it. As I navigated my way from engineering into management roles, I still never got excited about the technology itself.

So how was I effective as a technology business leader when I hated technology? I learned to use the very fact that I honestly hated technology as a core strength. And I focused on using that strength to add real business value. Here's what I mean.

I always felt that technology was too hard to use. It made people feel stupid when it didn't work right, and most of the time it didn't work right. It annoyed me.

As I climbed the ranks from sales engineer, to product marketing manager, to VP, GM, and CEO, I always focused on where the technology met the humans—and how to make that part work better and be less annoying.

I dealt directly with the technology as little as possible. I didn't spend time and energy trying to be more technical, because it was not a strength of mine (even though this is what my technology-oriented managers said they expected from me). Instead, I focused on what was a strength and source of energy for me—my understanding and caring about how to help humans work more effectively with technology.

So I focused my teams on making the product install better and the demo easier. I watched how people used our products. I learned where they got stuck and understood how they were thinking about the task at hand.

We made sure the products did what they were supposed to do in the way that the user expected. I also made sure that the business processes surrounding the technology were good for humans. We cleaned up things like sales presentations, partner contracts, distributor packaging, and license agreements. I sold my management on the fact that my leading this effort was more important to our business than my becoming more technical.

As it turns out, there was real value in making technology less annoying for humans! So I was succeeding, by using (1) my authentic dislike of technology and (2) my strengths in understanding what motivates and drives people to act in particular ways.

These people-oriented strengths also gave me the ability to build great teams and get them aligned and focused to achieve a common purpose. I had both the guts to make organizational changes and the intuition to get the right people into the right roles. I had strong skills to clarify strategies and turn them into realistic, effective action plans.

Thrive More at Work

By focusing on what I was really good at and what energized me, and by building strong teams to reinforce my weaker points, I was leading in a way that was true to myself. So it wasn't painful, and it created great success over and over again.

I figured out how to be really successful as a business leader *and* get a lot more enjoyment and a stronger sense of personal satisfaction and purpose in my well-paying, corporate, technology job. Life got better. Even my family noticed;

they would say things like, "It seems like you are actually enjoying your work; what happened?"

You Are at a Crossroads Now— You Have a Choice

Early on in your career you pay dues. We all do. You take the best job available, you roll up your sleeves, and you work really hard. You work long hours on sometimes stupid and thankless projects. And you tend to be consumed by the work. Your career "strategy" is more about reacting to opportunities that come along than planning what job you are going to do next and why. If you react successfully, you get ahead. You get some wins, some promotions, and some higher pay.

But then you reach a point where you decide that life should be better than this. You decide you want to do work that you *want* to do. You want to contribute real value to the business, but you want to get recognized for it. And you want to get some genuine satisfaction from your work. You want to make a difference. You don't want to give up your whole life for your work. You want your work to fit into your life so that your life works.

Basically, you don't want to work so hard for so little in return.

You notice that some people have broken out. They started where you were, but now they are in bigger jobs, making more money, and having more impact on the business. And they even seem kind of happy.

Now you are at the crossroads. "Do I continue to work hard and take the opportunities that come my way? Will I be *discovered* soon? Or should I do something on purpose to get more of what I want from my work?"

Take Your Real Self to Work

A big part of feeling unfulfilled and unhappy at work comes from feeling like you can't be your real self at work. It's really painful to have to put yourself through a personality lobotomy each morning, to turn yourself into someone else—your "work self"—just to go to work.

It is very draining. It takes a huge amount of energy to be that other person. I used to feel this, trying to be a "technology person." Think about how much more effective you could be at your job if you could use all of your energy on your work instead of spending a significant amount of it coping with the fact that you hate it.

How can you make your job be a source of energy—not a drain—so you will be extra-good at it and enjoy it more? How can you put yourself in the very best position to excel?

This starting point and foundation for big success is rooted in some ageless wisdom that can't be avoided or improved upon.

Figure Out What You're Really Good at, Then Do That

Manage your circumstances to ensure you'll be doing what you are naturally good at most of the time.

It starts with being clear about who you really are and then spending more and more of your time being that person and taking *that* person to work every day. Look for where your energy multiplies and go there. Avoid what drains it.

KEY INSIGHT: *If you play to your core strengths, you will be much more successful (because you are using your strengths) and feel far more satisfied in your work (because you are using your strengths).*

Don't Take Your Strengths for Granted

First, you need to figure out what your natural strengths are. This is not easy to do, because as humans we tend to take our natural strengths for granted. Your natural strengths are the things that come easily to you—the things you are really good at but require little effort. Because these things are easy for you, they don't feel very impressive. But you look at someone else who is good at something you find difficult, and you say, "Wow—now *that* is impressive!"

What you have to understand is that others are looking at the things *you* do with ease and saying, "Wow—now *that* is impressive!"

The first and biggest hazard of taking your strengths for granted is that you waste too much time trying to fix your weaknesses. As humans we tend to focus on the things we are not good at. I don't believe in investing in fixing weaknesses. It is a waste of time and energy, especially compared to building on strengths.*

Think about it this way. If you invest one unit of energy in building on a natural strength, you will get a certain return. If you invest that same one unit of energy on fixing a weakness, you will get a much smaller return—because you are not good at it! Why waste your time? Building on your strengths has a much bigger payoff.

If, for example, you are not naturally analytical, don't waste years trying to become analytical; focus instead on how to use your communication and conflict resolution strengths. If you are very technical or a master with data but you are not a future thinker, you are not going to become one. Instead, surround yourself with people who are and build on your organizational and process strengths.

The second big hazard of taking your strengths for granted is that you may not fully use them. So you miss an opportunity to excel. What better way to stand out and accomplish remarkable things than to work in the area of your greatest strengths? This also makes work much less painful and more fun. You succeed all the time, and it feels easy. The crowds cheer. You're not killing yourself, because you are working where you have real energy. And you're adding real value to the business.

Your Strengths Are in Plain Sight for Everyone but You

Natural strengths are not things like being good at supply chain management or business planning—those are skills. The strengths are underneath.

> **KEY INSIGHT:** *You need to find the essence of WHY you are good at what you are good at. This is where the real you comes in.*

---

*I want to point out the difference between a weakness and a behavior problem. A weakness is *not being good at something.* Not being analytical or not being strategic is a weakness. Being a jerk is a behavior problem. Behavior problems impede your ability to work with people. It is worth fixing behavior problems.

The real you is good at things like: decisiveness, empathy, ability to get to the core of a complex problem, working through conflict, taking action, being analytical, winning people over, competition, finding common ground, rationalizing lots of inputs, seeing the future, understanding how systems and organizations work, thinking strategically, executing and implementing, and connecting people. These are things that can be applied to any job.

Figure Out What Your Strengths Are

It's really hard to do this completely on your own. Interviewing people who know you, asking them what they think you are good at, helps expose some of the things you are likely taking for granted. And personality assessments and profiles can also provide really useful input. I have listed some of these tools in "Self-Assessments" in the Resources section on page 267.

Follow Your Energy

In your heart, you know when you feel really good and energized about your work and when you feel bored, tortured, and drained.

Think about a time when you were at the top of your game, a time when you were excited about your work, getting great results, and the crowds were cheering. Use that example to really focus on what gives you energy and the kinds of thinking, communicating, planning, and working that were involved. This will lead you to your natural strengths.

As an example, in my case I realized that I got a lot more energy from organizing, developing, and motivating teams than I did from technology roadmaps. I enjoyed leading and communicating more than managing sales execution on a month-by-month basis. Over my career, I tuned my job to put myself in a position to use my greatest strengths and built my teams of amazing people (to which I will be forever grateful for their work and support) to cover the rest.

When you follow your energy and work where you have natural strengths, you will find yourself feeling much more satisfied in your work.

Your Job Description Is Not a Life Sentence

We often tend to accept our job descriptions as as-written and unchangeable. Realizing that you don't need to do this is one of the keys to breaking out. You need to take control of redefining your job description to give yourself an advantage and a chance to enjoy your work more. If you focus on your natural strengths instead of the content of the work, you can tune your job description over time to put yourself in a position to thrive.

The good news is that you don't need to walk away from your paycheck, or even to get a different job, to feel more satisfied about your work.

KEY INSIGHT: *You have the power to renegotiate the contract of your work to better suit your strengths.*

Change Your Job without Changing Your Job

Once you have your strengths in focus, you need to think about how you can tune your job to put yourself in your "power alley" more of the time.

Here's an example of two different people I knew with different natural strengths who hated the same job!

They were both project managers. One was in a media production firm and the other was in a food-service logistics business. Neither really cared personally about the product they were working on, and they both had lots of annoying stuff to deal with. They felt unfulfilled, and on some days, they truly hated their jobs.

I found it fascinating that these were two different people in the same situation with two different sets of gifts and dislikes. The really interesting thing as I watched them each build their career was that it was not changing the content of the business or product that made them feel happier and more fulfilled—it was tuning their roles to suit their strengths.

Mari had a real gift for analysis and process but did not like giving presentations or arguing with people. In her mind she hated her job because she had to deal with difficult, annoying people all the time.

Josh was very insightful and empathetic and had a natural ability to engage and motivate people. But he was not naturally detail oriented, and he did not like tracking every minute logistical issue. In his mind, he hated his job because he felt stuck in the weeds.

Suit Your Strengths and Minimize Your Dislikes

Here is what happened. Over time, Mari was able to negotiate with her manager to take on a broader role to support all the project managers by improving the overall processes, creating templates for the production workflows, managing client needs and data, and so on. Building on her analysis and writing strengths, she was able to add real value to the business by creating infrastructure, processes, and efficiencies. And over time she needed to deal less and less with annoying people.

Josh went in the other direction. He decided to negotiate for new, highly politically challenging projects that spanned organizations and needed publicity. In those projects he made sure to staff detailed logistics experts. By building on his people strengths, he enabled the business to achieve significant outcomes on the biggest, messiest programs that required lots of hand-holding and finesse with vendors and clients. And over time he was able to spend less time in the weeds personally.

If Josh and Mari had not renegotiated their jobs, they would have gotten stuck in roles that they didn't like and were not great at. By renegotiating the content of their jobs, they both were able to put themselves in a position to excel for the business and in their careers.

Modifying your job doesn't happen overnight; it requires some effort and patience. But the payoff can be enormous. You can go from hating your job and feeling stuck to feeling good about your work and proud of what you deliver. And you can often do this without changing jobs, just by following your energy and tuning your job to take more and more advantage of your natural strengths.

An old colleague I recently ran into put it very well. When his manager expressed concern that his job had become more narrow, his response was, "I love my job. I am doing exactly what I am really good at. It's taken me twenty years to get all the stuff I suck at out of my job description."

Today you may need to gut your way through a job that does not use your natural strengths. But the lesson here is that you don't need to tolerate that forever!

Renegotiate Your Job

Think about how you can modify your job to take greater advantage of your personal core strengths. Remember, your job is a contract with your company. But make sure that in the negotiation, you are not talking about what you *want*. You need to *offer value*. If you go to your manager and say, "I want you to change my job so that I can do more of what I like," that will not go over well. You need to describe why it's good for the company to change how you do your job. As long as you can show you are doing things that add value to the business, you have the opportunity to renegotiate your contract over time—and you should be doing this.

It Is Up to You to Put Yourself in a Job Where You Can Thrive

All the highly successful people I have interviewed about this have had a moment in their career when they decided to put themselves in their power alley—to use their strengths and work where they had the most energy. They decided it was important to thrive. They redefined the terms under which they were willing to work. They stopped trying to do their job as it was defined for them, focused on what they were really good at, and worked with other people to cover the areas they were not good at.

Once you do this you will be surprised at how good this is for your company, how much more you can deliver, how impressed people will be, and how irrelevant your weaknesses become.

Your Choices

At any point you have three choices. If your job is not working for you, you can

1. Do nothing about it—make no change—stay there, be stuck.

2. Change the nature of your current job to be more successful and enjoyable.

3. Change your job.

Most of this book will center around #2, because #1 you can pretty much do without reading a book, and there are plenty of books out there to help you with #3. But also, if you do want to get a new job to make your life better, it's important to understand how doing #2 really works. That way you can make sure that your new job will be right for you and that you will thrive doing it.

Caveat #1: Get Outside Your Comfort Zone

Although it's a great strategy to build your career on your strengths, it's also important to challenge yourself. Learning new things that don't come easily improves your life skills. It gives you experience pushing through fear and self-imposed limits. It trains you be more purposeful. It keeps you humble. It makes you more well rounded. All this combines to make your strengths even stronger.

For example, I knew a young man gifted in math and science who challenged himself in public speaking and athletics (which he was frankly pretty bad at). But from this, he developed skills in communication, teamwork, and competition, and gained self-confidence that helped him thrive and stand out later in his medical career as a doctor and researcher.

Also, when you push beyond your known strengths, there is a chance you could develop a new skill or discover a new strength. So keep learning, but *don't try to make a living doing things you're not naturally good at.* It's just too hard. Challenge yourself for personal growth and fun, but earn your living doing work you can easily thrive at.

Caveat #2: Develop Communication Skills

If you lack natural strengths in communications, you can't simply not communicate. You don't need to master it or love it, but you do need to do it. Communicating is the one skill area that is worth everyone's investing in and improving on, even if it is not a core strength.

Your strategy for success will be threefold:

1. Maximize your strengths. This is still your best and strongest way to excel. You will make your greatest contributions (and earn your living) in your areas of natural strengths.

2. Force yourself to practice interacting and communicating even though it won't be your main contribution. You will improve with practice (and

it will get less painful, I promise). There is lots of advice for how to start and practice communicating in the LOOK Better and CONNECT Better sections of this book.

3. Partner with people whom you trust to help you in critical interactions and communications. There is some specific advice on this in chapter 14, Selling Your Ideas.

* * *

The Hard (and Important) Part

As much as we all crave someone to tell us what we should be when we grow up or to discover us and put us in the perfect job, it doesn't happen. Understanding your strengths at a core level is not easy to do, and it takes real time. But that investment of effort will give you a better roadmap to a successful, fulfilling career than anything else can.

You shouldn't be killing yourself working. It's up to you to tune and re-negotiate your job over time to better suit your strengths. If you simply leave this to the natural course of events, it will *not* happen. Jobs don't rewrite themselves just to suit you. It's a negotiation. Figure out how to align your strengths with something the business needs, and then make it happen for yourself over time.

Next . . . Don't deliver too much excellent work.

5. They Shoot Workhorses, Don't They?

Be Recognized for Getting Important Work Done . . . But Not for Doing It All Personally

Are you known for being someone who always delivers? Do you do a good job of everything that is asked of you? And does the work just keep getting piled on?

You may think you are being highly valued for the amazing amount of work that you deliver. And you may be. But let's be clear: you are being valued as a workhorse, not as leader to be promoted.

Being a Workhorse Will Get You Stuck

If you are known as being someone who can always take on more work personally, guess what? You will keep getting more work. After all, why would anyone be motivated to promote you and lose their workhorse?

The tricky part, and the reason why people fall into the workhorse trap, is that it feels like you are doing the right thing. You are working very hard. You are giving it your all. Isn't that supposed to be a good thing?

Yes, it's important to deliver results, but you need to work on the right things, in the right ways, and at the right level if you want to get ahead. The reason you are not getting anywhere as a workhorse is that you are working the *wrong way*. You are keeping yourself too busy to add value to the business over and above your personal work output. This can be a hazard both for the individual contributor who never looks up from her work and for the people-manager who can't let go of the work.

As a workhorse, you miss the opportunity to focus on Ruthless Priorities because you never give yourself the time to think about them, let alone do them. You also run the risk of getting burned out.

In this chapter we'll talk about the most common traps that lure you into workhorse mode, how to recognize them, and how to escape! You'll learn how you can change your way of working to deliver results and add more value to the business—so you stand out as a leader, not just as a workhorse.

How Leaders Emerge from Workhorses

Leaders emerge because they are seen to get the work done through their leadership, not by their personal effort.

I know an excellent example of such a leader who went from being initially fully consumed personally by an enormous hairball of a task, to ultimately solving the problem by leading. In doing so he stood out to a wide array of executive management as a high-potential future leader, not as a workhorse. Here is the story.

There was an inventory crisis. It was a bad one. We were off by an order of magnitude between what we could ship and what was necessary to support the business.

Sales managers, sales reps, partners, and customers from all over the world were calling to scream at us—me in particular. They had a point. This was indeed an ugly situation, caused by many factors, and it was going to take us almost three months to build enough inventory to meet the business demand.

The guy I had in charge of inventory came into my office the day the shortage was first communicated and the phones were ringing off the hook, and said, "Forward all the calls and emails to me. It will help me manage the situation if I am seeing all the information. I will handle this so you don't have to take the calls." *Wow. OK.* He took all this flack personally for a few days and did a great job at shielding me and the other executives from it.

The first week, through his personal attention and engagement with the various angry parties, he got the screaming to die down, and the sales regions came to believe that their needs were being addressed fairly, even though it was not really satisfactory. As far as I was concerned, this manager had solved the problem and was doing a great job (mostly because no one was yelling at me). But he was personally working round the clock, managing a relentless stream of emails and phone calls to do it. He was in workhorse mode.

By the next week, he had created an inventory priority request system. He came to me to review the business logic for prioritizing our stupidly few systems in the face of the huge demand. He asked me to coauthor an email to the regional executives, outlining how we prioritized requests for systems and the process for distributing them. In this email he described how each region was responsible for consolidating the issues that came in from new sales, existing customers, and partners. Then he ran a global meeting each week, to personally mediate the conflict and schedule the inventory distribution based on the regional rollups and the agreed priorities.

By the next week after that, he had built the set of prioritization rules into the system so that regional requests came in with specific ratings for each customer situation, and he was able to route the precious little inventory to the regions without even having the big screaming meeting at all.

The inventory crisis lasted for almost three months, but it consumed him for only three weeks. After that, the systems and communications he had created took hold, and it took a reasonable amount of his time to manage it and keep it running. He could get back to other things. And we continued to use the inventory management process that he created whenever the business had any kind of inventory shortage.

The Moral of This Story

If he had stayed in the first phase of handling all these requests personally (which all of the executives were happy enough with, because we were not the ones getting yelled at), he would have gotten the job done, been recognized as a hero, and been rewarded for hard work above and beyond the call of duty.

But he would not have been recognized as a leader. He would have been recognized as a workhorse.

If he had stayed in workhorse mode for the whole three months, he would have received a lot of credit for working really hard and delivering good results, but he would have not stood out as someone who was ready to step up to a bigger job.

But by demonstrating his ability to get his arms around the crisis, create systems, and continue to improve the result while spending less and less personal time at it, he became recognized as an effective leader and manager—someone who could take on bigger things without getting fully consumed. He was promoted soon after that, and the value he created and the leadership he demonstrated in that inventory crisis definitely played a role in his getting ahead.

Workhorse Traps and Escape Routes

You are already too busy to do anything more. So if you want to get out of workhorse mode, what can you do? Where do you start?

First and foremost, you need to give yourself some breathing room and some thinking time.

Start Thinking

Most people say they would be better at their job if they had more time to think.

So what would you think about? For starters, you need to think about how to get the work done in a way that doesn't fully consume you. But the most important thing is to start thinking! Actually schedule some time to think. Start with two hours. Then try to schedule two hours every week.

If you never give yourself the permission and time to step above the work-horse way of working and you stay overbusy, you will remain stuck and you will continue to fail to add real value to the business.

When you start your thinking, a good place to get started is to look for low-value, time-consuming activities. Identify your most soul-sucking, chaotic, or repetitive work activities. These are the workhorse traps. Use your thinking time to make it a point to either avoid them or to fix them on purpose.

Trap: Lack of Effective Communication

Think about how much time is spent in your organization clarifying things, answering questions, revisiting decisions that have been made, clearing up mis-understandings, and generally just discussing things a lot, over and over and over again.

To get out of workhorse mode, think instead about creating a communi-cation process that would eliminate most of these questions, emails, discus-sions, and meetings. Really think through who is involved and where the misunderstandings occur. What information would you need to provide, how often, in what form, and to whom in order to reduce the time spent in tedious clarifications?

If you do this, you will not only free up your own time, but save a lot of time for many other people and be seen as adding real value.

Trap: Random Emergencies

Unplanned work comes from all directions, from your team, your peers, and very often from your boss. A workhorse will have the tendency to take on each new crisis in turn and add the work to their current workload. Unplanned crises or information fetching and polishing exercises that take up most of your time, get you stuck in workhorse mode.

First, you need to step back and assess the unplanned crises. List the last ten. Where did they come from? Rank them in order of importance. How many of them were truly important? What do the important ones have in common? Are there any proactive things you can do to prevent some of them from happening? Is there enough commonality in some of them where creating a new process can help? Can you develop new strategies or tools to deal with the unique ones more quickly? Can you push back on the ones that are not really important?

You also need to be realistic about how much time this unplanned work *should take*. Let's face it; you can't make them all go away. So you need to block out a certain amount of your time for the truly important, unplanned work. How much time is it in your world? Is it 10 percent, 30 percent, 50 percent? You can't book 100 percent of your time on "your day job" and expect to just squeeze in random emergencies. Be realistic. Leave some room. Then you will be able to do the heroic work when necessary without getting stuck in workhorse mode.

Trap: Team Downsizing without Work Downsizing

Another situation that lures you into workhorse mode is when your team gets smaller but none of the work goes away. In the beginning, yes, you will likely need to take on the extra work until you understand it, but you need to avoid the temptation to stay in that mode forever after.

> **KEY INSIGHT:** *I say "temptation" because staying in workhorse mode is, in many ways, easier than putting in the extra effort and strategic thought to change the way you work. It takes real commitment and effort to create a new way of working and to take the necessary risks to negotiate a new way of working.*

As we talked about in chapter 1 on productive laziness (Be Less Busy), in a way it is lazier to stay overbusy than it is to proactively put in the effort to strategically manage an overwhelming workload.

It's important to realize that you should not just accept *fewer people, more work* as the way things are indefinitely. If the smaller team is a permanent condition, you must reset the priorities and the workload. At some point you need to step up and build a different and better way of getting the work done, or you will be allowing what should be a temporary condition to send you into workhorse mode, long term. Then you're stuck.

Trap: Failing to Delegate

If you find yourself overbusy because you are jumping in to do work your team should be doing, or covering for them because their work is not good enough, you will get consumed by it.

There are several reasons failing to delegate well will get you stuck. We'll talk about all of them and how to master delegating in chapter 7, Delegate or Die. But one thing is sure. Failing to delegate effectively will keep you locked in workhorse mode. The workload is unsustainable. If this is an issue for you, you need to solve it if you want to get ahead. How can you get promoted if you have not built a team capable of doing not only their own work, but also some of yours?

You must master delegating—full stop. It is never the right choice to jump in and do the work your team should be doing as a steady-state way of working. You need to either train the people or change the people. Doing their work is not your job. You need to *pull your team up* and make them more capable so you can free up your time, get out of workhorse mode, and work on higher-value things.

Don't Get Burned Out

Working really hard for a long time without enough recognition, payoff, or advancement takes a toll. I have seen many people who have remained in work-horse mode for many years. The longer you stay there, the more likely you are to get stuck there because it becomes what you are known for. Once you are known as a longtime workhorse, it becomes even harder to get known for some-thing else. Eventually you accept that this is the way life is, and you lose the will to break out of it.

The ghost of workhorse future: "Make a change now so you don't end up here!"

But even if you are here, it's not too late. You have more control than you think. You may have a bigger hole to climb out of and you may be discouraged and feel stuck, but you can use the ideas in this chapter and the rest of book to break out.

Go on Vacation

Another trait of the workhorse is to put off enjoying life until all the work is done.

In the United States, many companies have a maximum amount of vacation days that employees can accrue. If you don't use your vacation days over a few years, you reach the maximum and stop accruing them.

People regularly used to tell me with pride that they had maxed out on vacation days and were no longer accruing them because they had not taken a vacation in years. I was supposed to be really impressed at how dedicated they were to their work. It was actually a neon sign on their forehead that read "Workhorse."

KEY INSIGHT: *No one cares how hard you work. It's about results. Not taking vacations is not something to be proud of nor is it a precursor to great success. This is really only a sign of being so out of control at work that you are demonstrating you are someone who can't plan and prepare enough to take a week off.*

* * *

The Hard (and Important) Part

When you are a workhorse, people value you for your work output; they don't value *you*. They don't care how hard you work; they only care that the work gets done. Your company can absorb an unlimited amount of work from you.

It can feel scary to break out of workhorse mode if your value has been associated with amazing throughput. But just keep in mind, if you could be replaced with a black box that they could insert the work into and it would come out complete, that would be fine with them.

But this is actually good news. It doesn't matter how much time you personally spend at the work, as long as it gets done. To break out of workhorse mode, you need to invent systems and processes that use less of your personal time to handle the work. Show that you can get the work done. But also show that you can free yourself from being overwhelmed by the work. When you get above the work to do higher-value things, this is when you will get noticed.

Next . . . Are you sure you still know
what high performance means?

6. The Level Dilemma

Each Time You Step Up a Level, What It
Means to Be Good at Your Job Changes

Here's the big issue: to be a great manager, you must *want* to rise above the work.

You must *want* to do the *managerial tasks* more than you want to do the work you used to do. You must understand that your job changes dramatically each time you step up a level. It's not just a different title and pay scale. It's a different job.

When you step up, it's not about doing the work, or even worrying so much about the content of the work anymore. It's about growing an organization beneath you that can get the work done even better than you could do it. It's about figuring out how to do things better when the world and budgets are set against you, as we talked about in the last two chapters. Your value is in developing strategy, people, and teams, not in delivering the work personally. Do you want *that* job? What does it mean to be good at that job?

The Value Shifts

Here's why it's so tricky and why so many people fail to rise to the next level successfully. When you were an individual worker, you valued—and you were valued for—doing an excellent job at the work: the knowledge, details, tasks, and so on. Being expert at the work defined your value. But as a leader who has stepped up, you need to associate your value with different stuff. If you don't start to associate your value with the higher-level managerial and leadership work, you will automatically gravitate back to the detail, because that is where you feel the value is. You'll keep working at the wrong level, and you'll fail to do an effective job as a leader.

What Does Competence Mean Now?

What makes you a high-performing individual worker is not the same stuff that makes you a high-performing manager. And what makes you a high-performing manager is not the same stuff that makes you a high-performing business leader.

When you step up to manage people, or to manage managers, or to manage a business, you need to associate your competence with performing at the next level of leadership, not the former level of work or the former level of management tasks.

You Are Not the Expert Anymore

The trap: You like being the expert. You have always been the expert. But now you have experts working for you, so you feel the need to be as smart as (or even smarter than) they are. You might even work extra hours to keep on top of all the detail in addition to whatever new stuff you are working on as the leader. It's important, or perhaps even fun, for you to invest the extra effort because you feel like you will lose credibility and the respect of your team if you don't understand the work as well as they do.

KEY INSIGHT: *You don't need to know everything you used to know about the content and the detail. In fact, even trying to know as much as your people do about the guts of the work will block your success as a leader.*

Here are the problems with this approach:

- You are investing energy you can't afford in the wrong place. (It's not your job anymore.)

- You fail to do the necessary managerial and leadership work that supports your team to add value to the business. (This is your new job.)

- You fail to build credibility with your team as their leader.

- You fail to grow people in your team.

I was talking to a director in a manufacturing business who shared a really great way of thinking about this. She said, "Your team needs to make you bigger."

In other words, if you try to stay involved in everything your team does, *you* don't get bigger. Your contribution does not get bigger. You are still constraining the amount of value you're adding to what you alone can process. You need to lead a team that makes your overall contribution much bigger. If you don't enable and allow your team to make you bigger, you shouldn't have a team.

Step *Up* and *Out*

Each time you step up to a bigger job, you need to let go of more content and more detail. Think of stepping *up* as stepping *out* of content and detail and needing to push more content and detail down to the level below you.

Rise Above the Work

Your team wants you to be a good leader; they will respect your leadership endeavors more than they will respect your trying to keep doing their work. They would prefer that you get out of their way, actually.

Remember, no one cares how hard you work. It's about business outcomes. Your value now is about how well you perform your new leadership responsibilities. How well do you identify the most important business outcomes to drive? How well do you redefine the workload to have the highest impact, and how well do you build a team that can deliver? Your success is no longer about your ability to know all the details and excel at the work.

Missing the Level Transition Will Cost You

People who don't make the transition to work at the right level when they step up wreak other havoc as well. In addition to spending too much time personally working at a lower level, they

- End up competing with their subordinates about who is smarter

- Continue to torture their team for inappropriate amounts of detail

- Waste everyone's time doing deep dives into content

- Develop a culture around being a brilliant hero rather than building a high-performing team

- Fail to hire smart people beneath them because they are threatened by people knowing more than they do about the content

- Fail to develop capacity in the team to do more

- Fail to develop future leaders

- Lose high performers

- Miss the opportunity to set strategic direction

OK, So What Should You Be Doing at Your Level?

For some people the issue is not being afraid to let go of the detail but the daunting fact that they don't know what to do otherwise. The job underneath them is the one they know how to do.

So the big question is, *If I don't do what I used to be good at, what do I actually DO now?* Really think about that. If you stop doing *any* of the same work you did yesterday, and now 100 percent of your time is free to do your new next-level management work—what exactly should you be doing?

In some ways it is easier (or more fun) to just keep focused on the work and to think you are adding value by staying involved in the content and pitching in, than it is to figure out what new work you should be doing—things you may not be as comfortable with initially.

How to Figure Out What to Do

I once worked with a business leader in a large logistics corporation who was not getting this. He did not make the level change. He kept competing with a highly capable subordinate, stepping in personally to do complicated, visible work that he should have delegated. When we talked about why he kept doing this, it became clear that he did not know how else to show what value he was adding. If his team was as capable as he was, what was his job?

One of my mentors taught me something important: if, as a leader, you are not sure what to do, talk to *everybody*. You must regularly talk to the individuals who are doing the work and who are closest to the customers if you want to know what is actually happening in your business. This is also how you learn what your job needs to be. In all my executive jobs, I budgeted time every week to talk to the individuals doing the work. I relished the customer visits, not for the customer contact but for the ride in the car with the sales rep. Talking to the people doing the work shows you the way forward.

Some leaders resist doing this for two basic reasons: (1) they feel like they are going around the managers who report to them, or (2) their ego tells them, "I am a big shot, so I don't talk to the people doing the work; I only talk to managers."

Stay Connected to Reality

You can never rely solely on the information that comes up through your managers. It's not that they are hiding things intentionally, but you'll never get the whole picture if you don't get a steady stream of unfiltered feedback from the individuals doing the work. It's also important to talk to the direct consumers of the work. It's not a problem if you just make it part of the culture with your managers that you are going to spend time talking to individuals. As long as you don't start directly assigning work to individuals without involving their manager, the managers are not offended or concerned by your having the conversations.

Once this manager started talking to individuals, he realized some important things that he just wasn't seeing before. He learned that there were three different project teams in his organization that were duplicating each other's work. He didn't see this because his managers weren't talking to each other about it! He learned that the customer satisfaction survey scores were high only because the questions were tuned to get the right answers, not the real opinions of the customers.

None of this information was coming up through his direct staff. It wasn't that his managers were doing a bad job or withholding critical information on purpose. But even with the best intentions all around, you can never get a full picture when you rely solely on information translated by others (remember playing Telephone?).

Once he started seeing this stuff, the lightbulb went on. He knew what his job was. He saw where he should be adding value. He needed to fix organization issues. He needed to build quality and reality into the customer satisfaction program. The next time he was called on for a detailed presentation about what his team did, instead of doing it himself, as he had in the past, he delegated it to his high performer—because now he was too busy doing his real job!

Use the critical insight you gain from talking to individuals about what's really happening to improve the business—BUT resist the temptation to jump in to personally fix or change things at the wrong level. Your job is to manage the organization. Figure out what needs to be fixed, improved, created, or stopped and delegate the implementation to the people who need to do it.

Working *On* the Business versus *In* the Business

Being stuck in the content and detail is working *in* the business. Rising above the content to lead and build capability in your team is working *on* the business. Essentially, you want to spend more time *thinking* and less time *doing*. If you are spending all your time doing, you are probably not working *on* the business.

Here are some ideas for what you should be focusing on as a leader at the right level to work *on* the business.

- Build a plan to drive the overall strategy for your team and its contribution to the business. Look for game-changing opportunities.

- Clarify Ruthless Priorities. Tune everyone's workload to ensure that they deliver on the most important things.

- Ensure that there is strategic alignment of your team, peers, and boss with priorities and values.

- Assess your organization's fitness for what it needs to do, and make changes, train, and/or upgrade talent where necessary.

- Create systems and frameworks to execute, track, and measure the work so you can feel comfortable that you know what is getting done without diving into the details. See also chapter 7, Delegate or Die.

- Create a specific learning agenda for your team, such as understanding the financial realities of the business, getting closer to customers, or competitive awareness and positioning.

- Develop talent. Help your team become better leaders and support them. Focus on the development of their top talent.

- Improve communication inside and outside your organization.

- Find ways to steadily reduce the cost of things you do every year to make room for new things. See also chapter 8, Better with Less.

- Continually make connections outside your direct organization to create positive visibility for your team and create a broader base of support.

Quick Check—Do You Like This Level of Work?

- If you have a leadership job, the preceding list describes the kinds of the things you should be doing.

- If you are interviewing for a big job, these are the things you should be talking about.

- If you can't get more excited about this type of work than you are about being the expert and doing the same work that the team does, you shouldn't step up to the next level. There is nothing wrong with this. You can have a highly successful and satisfying career without being a people manager. This level check is a good test to decide if you really want to be a manager or not.

By the way, having some mentors who are well versed in working at a higher level can be invaluable if you have any blind spots around the kinds of things on this list. We'll talk about mentors in chapter 15, Get Help. Mentors can point you to the new parts of your job that you should be doing but that might not ever occur to you.

Make Your Team More Capable

Much of what working at the right level—and working *on* the business—leads to is making your team more capable. As a leader, your job is not just about managing the work output of your team. Of course you need to make sure that the work gets delivered, but that is only entry stakes. That is not standout leadership behavior. Your real job as a leader is to make sure your team gets better and more capable over time.

Think about it this way: on your first day as a manager, your team has the capability to deliver at a certain capacity in terms of their general output and the level, quality, complexity, and innovation of what they can deliver.

If after a year you have delivered all the work you had committed to, but your team is still performing at the same capacity, you have not done your job as a leader. You have managed the work, but you have not added value to the business by increasing the capacity of the individuals on your team or their performance as a team.

And if you met your commitments by taking on huge amounts of work personally at the wrong level, if you are working at the same level as your team, you never stood a chance of growing the capability of your team.

KEY INSIGHT: *If you don't grow capacity over time, as the business gets harder, you and your team will no longer be qualified at your jobs.*

An Example from the Services Industry

Natalie was a regional director for a services organization. She found that she needed to be the one to personally review all client proposals before they went out because frequently they were incomplete or contained some embarrassing errors. This proposal review task was taking up huge amounts of her time. It needed to be done and it was important that it be done correctly, because these proposals were what brought the revenue in.

Natalie was overwhelmed by this task, doing all the work personally— reviewing and modifying proposal after proposal. She felt like she was doing the right thing because she was prioritizing a revenue-generating activity. Natalie fell into the trap of working at the wrong level, thinking, "I am the only one who can do this right, so I need to do all of them."

Although she was able to get each proposal up to the necessary standard, and many resulted in revenue, she was failing to add value to the business at the right level in three ways:

1. She was not leading the business to deliver even more proposals by creating a better and more efficient system for doing so. So she was failing to enable the business to grow revenue. She was delivering work instead.

2. She was wasting time she could have been spending on client sales engagements, so she was failing to improve customer relationships or to develop new opportunities or to help close a higher percentage of business.

3. She was failing to develop talent in her team so they would be able to step up and take over the proposal work they should be doing.

Here is what Natalie did to start working at the right level and add more value to the business.

She created new processes for proposal creation and review, by taking these steps:

1. She created a checklist that covered 50 percent of the things she consistently needed to change.

2. The checklist was distributed to everyone with a new requirement that the checklist had to be completed and submitted with the proposal.

3. She created a template for an accurate proposal that an administrative assistant could check against to make sure that the proposal was complete and structured properly and that the spelling and grammar were corrected before it got to her.

4. She asked her team to develop standardized descriptions of common work, which she approved only once.

5. She modified the approval process to have most sections reviewed and signed off by the accountable person on her team.

6. She found a financial partner to review the financial and legal aspects of each contract.

7. Now Natalie needed to personally review only the section that described the overall business relationship and value proposition for the deal, to tune the sales language to be most compelling—one of her key strengths.

She was now working at the right level. She was working *on* the business. She created a system to improve the overall process and freed up her own time so she could spend more of her time selling to new prospects and clients—growing the business.

This seems like a simple change, but it's important to think about it in terms of level. Natalie had differentiated the elements of the sales and proposal process that needed to be done at *her team's level* from the additional value that she should be adding at *her level*.

What else could Natalie be doing at the right level? She could develop the strategy for the region. She could assess the service offerings and the sales process. She could assess her team and both train and upgrade talent to the level necessary to grow the business. She could recruit new partners to expand the reach of her business, or she could implement new business arrangements with current partners to increase revenue or profits.

If she had remained in the role of being the "expert" at creating the best proposals, she would have missed the opportunity to do her real job and add value at the right level to grow the capability of her team and grow the business.

Never Carry Detail Up

A good checkpoint for yourself is to make sure that you are never the one to carry detail up. Part of working at the right level is always to turn detail into higher-value information.

This may happen through summaries or abstractions, or it may happen by picking out one compelling, detailed example that tells the whole story to the next level up. But if you simply get detail from your team and then you share it with your boss, you are working at the wrong level.

What If Your Boss Is Guilty of Being Stuck in the Detail?

This is such a common problem, because there are many, many leaders out there who have never made the transition to embrace their higher-level leadership responsibilities. They have not let go of the content and the detail. This causes two big problems for you: First, as much as you are trying to work at the right level and never carry detail upward, you boss is versed in and demanding more detail than even you are involved with. So you appear to be caught off-guard. Second, your boss fails to create the value for the business required by working at his level.

Here are a few ideas.

1. Distract Your Boss from the Details

Help your boss see the necessary level she needs to transition to by proposing the kinds of measures she should be worried about. This will require you to think and work at your boss's level so that you can expose her to the right level of strategic thinking. (By the way, it's a good thing to work up a level.) Suggest some specific work that you see needs to be done at her level.

I knew a marketing VP in a nonprofit organization whose CFO was so hung up on numbers that if the VP had a ten-page strategic presentation with one two-by-two matrix containing four numbers, they would spend the entire hour talking about those four numbers. The VP's strategy with him: don't show him any numbers!

2. Articulate What Work Should Be Done at Your Level, Your Boss's Level, and Your Team's Level

Spell it out all at once. It is possible to educate your boss about work the organization needs her to be doing and at the same time show her the high-value work you are doing instead of being mired in the detail. Make it clear there is a difference between what you are doing and what your team is doing. It will become clear that she is jumping down two levels if you spell it out all at once and show her what needs to be done at her level. Inspire your boss to climb up and out too.

3. Focus the Discussion on the Desired Business Outcome

If you can drive more conversations to focus on key future desired outcomes instead of current work, the discussions and resulting actions will naturally gravitate to a less detailed, more strategic level. Discussions about current work are inherently more detailed and at a lower level than discussions about "Why is this important?" "What business outcome is this supporting?" and "Is that still the right outcome, or should we clarify the desired outcome?"

One Exception

There is a rare breed of successful executive that lives in the detail and *also* does the high-value leadership work successfully. This type of success is a freak of nature. These people are also so busy all the time that they have no appreciable life otherwise. It can work, but it is not something to aspire to. The vast majority of managers who try to hang on to the detail on the way up get stuck, fail to lead effectively, and fail to create enough business value.

* * *

The Hard (and Important) Part

No one will specifically instruct you how to change your job when you step up. You need to have your own plan to let go of the content and take on new leadership responsibilities. Don't try this without a mentor!

Don't get stuck leading an organization that can't grow (or can't live without you) because you misread the real requirements of what leadership is about at your level.

You need to be prepared emotionally for not being the expert any more and for finding your value elsewhere. You need to earn your team's respect with your leadership skills, not by trying to stay as smart as they are on the detail.

If you keep working at the wrong level, it will have a very high cost to your team, your business, and your career. Rise. Everybody up!

Next . . . You must get good at delegating
if you want to advance.

7. Delegate or Die

Don't Think of Delegating as Just Assigning Work;
Think of It as Building Value in Your Team

Why is delegating so hard? Usually, it's because you don't trust the person to deliver as well as you can. Or you don't want to lose control of how it's done. Or you think it will take too much time to show someone else how to do it.

Get over it. You will never add enough value to the business if you get stuck doing work for your team. It might be easier in the short term, but it's less effective in the long term, and it's unsustainable. That way of working will kill you. Effective delegating is a must.

Where's the Value?

Let's start with the basic math. If you have ten people working for you, you will create way more value for the company by developing ten people to step up and deliver at your level than by adding one more person—*you*—to step down to deliver at their level.

85

Let's do more math. If you have ten people working for you, you can attempt to be as technically smart and deep in the content as they are. But what happens if you manage a hundred people? Can you still stay as deep? What if it's a thousand? At some point it becomes impossible to stay as versed in the detail and the content as all the individuals in your organization.

But that is not even the point. The point is that you shouldn't even try, even with ten people. If you don't let go of the detail, you are missing the opportunity to do the higher-level job—that is, *your* job.

Think of Delegating as Building Value

KEY INSIGHT: *Don't think of delegating as just giving work to other people; think about it as making sure the highest-value work gets done at the right levels.*

Make sure you understand the difference between the right strategic work that should be done at your level and the work that should be done by your team. Don't fall into the trap of being helpful by pitching in to do the work. That is not your job.

Remember: you need to deliver business outcomes. Delegating is about developing the people on your team so they can step up to do the required work. If you delegate well, they become more valuable over time, and you free up your time so you can also become more valuable over time.

My "Big Break"

One of the things that I consider to be really lucky in my career was that in my first big management job, I was utterly incapable of jumping in and working down a level. Here is what happened.

I was offered a choice of running either the marketing organization or the R&D (software product development) organization.

Because I had spent most of my time in marketing, and my desired outcome was to be a general manager, I jumped at the chance to run R&D.

So there I was, running an R&D organization. Although my background was in engineering, I hadn't been an engineer for many years. I had no way of personally doing the work my team was doing or even trying to add value by advising them on how to do it better.

My "weakness"—my inability to jump in and do the work of my managers—became one of the luckiest accidents of my career. If I had taken the marketing role, I almost certainly would have jumped in and tried to "add value" to the work. I don't think I could have resisted (nor did I know that I should have resisted), because I was personally more experienced at some of the marketing stuff than anyone on the team. In the R&D role, I simply had no choice. I didn't understand and couldn't possibly do the work.

But because I was someone who was driven to add value, right out of the gate in my management career I was forced to find ways to work at the right level, to add value to the organization and the business, completely over and above the work that was being done in my organization. I had to quickly learn how to delegate without understanding the content, adding value personally, or losing control of the outcomes.

When I got my first performance review as the manager of this R&D team, I was a bit nervous because I didn't really understand my team's work at some significant depth; did my team think I was credible? As it turned out, several people on my team had given my boss the feedback that I was the best manager they had ever had.

Here I was thinking that I was in over my head because I didn't understand the content. But because I was doing the right stuff at the right level, as a manager I was succeeding in a big way for the business and the people. This was a big learning experience for me. There is really important and valuable management stuff to be done once you rise above the work.

Key Factors to Delegating Well

There are eight secrets to delegating effectively.

1. Resist Temptation—Don't Do the Work

We all get tempted to jump in and do the work ourselves, but it is never the right strategy long term.

Do you find yourself thinking any of the following?

- It's easier if I just do it myself.

- It will take less time to do it myself than if I try to teach someone to do it.

- I am better at this than they are.

- This is really important; it needs to turn out well. So I'll just do it myself.

- Damn, this isn't good enough, and the big presentation is tomorrow, so I will need to stay late and redo it.

One of the reasons that delegating is so hard is that at any given moment, it *is* easier to just do it yourself. You may even create some better outcomes, in the short term, by doing the work yourself. But you need to recognize that that is an unsustainable model, that you are failing to build a team that *can* do the work, and that team building is your job.

You are robbing value from the company both by using your pay grade to work at a lower level and by failing to get the necessary results out of the people you have employed to do it.

Too Much Work

If there is too much work to go around and you must do some of it yourself, you need to be really clear to yourself, your team, and your boss that you are making an exception to cover a short-term requirement.

If you make it clear that this is temporary, you leave the door open to either recruit additional resources later or to reprioritize and renegotiate the workload. But if you just silently take this on because it needs to get done, or let this become a steady-state way of working, you have slipped into workhorse mode, you are working at the wrong level, and you are stuck.

2. Get Over Any Guilt about It

Some people feel guilty or uncomfortable delegating. They feel like if they delegate too much, people will think they aren't doing anything. Get over it. And remember, by delegating you are freeing up your time to do *different* work, work that you need to be doing. While you are delegating, sell the benefit of that work to your team. Everyone wins.

I know I used to feel guilty delegating big ugly work—work that I personally thought was really hard—to the managers who worked for me. Why should I get off the hook and give this horrible job to someone else while I have a nice day? But I came to realize two important things:

1. By not delegating, my managers would perceive that I didn't trust them, because it would appear that I believed I needed to do their jobs myself.

2. *Ugly is in the eye of the beholder.*

> **KEY INSIGHT:** *This is where the magic of focusing on strengths and delegating come together. I realized that often this work felt so ugly to me because* I was bad at it. *Because I had built a team that reinforced my weaker areas, the stuff I thought was most ugly and difficult actually suited their strengths. So they were happy to do the work!*

For them it was fun, easy work. This is a huge win. You don't have to do the work that's ugly to you, and it gets done way better than you could have done it anyway. The people are perfectly happy to do it, and they can be proud of the outcome. Again, everyone wins.

Okay, sometimes the work is just ugly, and the person you are delegating it to thinks it's ugly too! I once had a wise mentor tell me that even in this case, if I kept the work myself, trying to be "nice," the manager who rightly owned the work would probably see this as a lack of trust. She'd be more upset by my getting into her work than by doing the ugly work herself. Also, it would keep me from doing the work I needed to be doing at my level. So I did delegate the ugly work, but offered a lot of thank-yous and recognition to the person I was asking to deal with the crap.

3. Don't Cover for Poor Work

Your job is not to cover for work by your team that is not good enough. Your job is to make sure you develop the required capability and capacity in your team to deliver excellent work. If you don't delegate the work that should be done by your team, you will end up working several jobs because you have failed to build the right, capable team (this is where the "or die" part of "delegate or die" happens).

Look at it this way: your boss wouldn't cover for you. For example, if you create a presentation for your boss that is not good enough, your boss is not going to work until midnight to redo it. He will either make you redo it or fire you and get someone who can do it well. If you are getting work from your team that is not good enough, it is up to you to pull your people up, not to take over and redo it yourself.

4. Don't Kill Your Planned Hires

If you are negotiating for open positions on your team, don't jump in personally to get the work done before they get there. Let some important stuff go undone, or get done poorly, so you make it clear that you really need the hire.

If you keep coming to the rescue—working evenings and weekends—you'll never get your hire approved. You'll only be proving that you don't *really* need that hire. And by the way, you are slipping into workhorse mode, working at the wrong level, and failing to build a capable team.

5. Keep Ownership of the Outcome

There are two elements of the delegation spectrum worth avoiding: micromanaging and abandonment.

Micromanaging happens when you get nervous that it won't come out right. So you meddle along the way. Leaders tend to do this in the parts of the work where they feel most comfortable and knowledgeable—where they are expert.

On the other end of the spectrum of pitfalls is abandonment. *Abandonment* is giving something over so completely that you do not even take ownership for the outcome—you just hope for the best. This is typical for work you hate or areas you don't know about. A savior comes to work for you. You are so happy you don't have to deal with this work personally that you just hand it over and don't even want to talk about it!

Being so hands-off in particular areas sends really weird signals to your team. They think the things you meddle in are important to you and the things you don't meddle in are not.

No matter how much (or how little) you know about the work you are delegating, you need to retain ownership of a successful outcome. If you are tempted to either micromanage or abandon the whole thing, the best approach is to set a clear desired outcome and then establish a set of intermediate outcomes and measures along the way.

This outcome-oriented approach allows you to retain ownership of the successful outcome, without either meddling or worrying that you don't know how to do the work yourself. You can feel comfortable that milestones are being hit along the way without managing all the detail or failing to take any responsibility at all.

6. Get More Comfortable

Getting good at delegating does not mean that you have to just learn to deal with the psychological issues of discomfort and loss of control and hope for the best.

> **KEY INSIGHT:** *You don't need to learn how to deal with the worry; you need to eliminate the need to worry!*

Let Them Define the Measures

When you delegate to someone, in your initial conversations, make the desired outcome and the time line really clear. Then ask *her* to come back to you with the plan and milestones. Ask her to define how she wants you to measure them.

When you let the person you delegate to define the measures and the milestones, often you will actually get a better, more aggressive, and complete plan than you would have come up with yourself. And the person will be more accountable to it.

7. Measure and Inspect

Another pitfall of delegating is not closing the loop on what you assigned and letting expected milestones go by unmet, without consequences, or get completed, without recognition. You need to let people know you are serious about commitments.

When you are good at delegating, you create frameworks and processes that feed you the information you need along the way, so you remain confident and comfortable that the work is getting done.

This is so important. If you find yourself assigning tasks but then absolutely hating "being the guy with the clipboard" who checks up on everything, then there is no follow-up, you fail to execute, and you will fail.

> **KEY INSIGHT:** *If you are not good at doing this tracking and reporting piece yourself, delegate it to someone who is naturally good at it!*

This tracking piece was not something I was particularly good at or enjoyed doing. So I always had someone on my team who would keep track of all the milestones we committed to and create the tracking process and templates to make the status easy for the team to update and for me to review. Having someone on my team who thrived on this type of follow-through was an enormous asset to my career success because my team always got things done as committed.

8. Always Be Teaching

The question you need to ask yourself if delegating doesn't work out right is whether the problem is a skill issue with the employee or an issue with your ability to delegate.

Always think of delegating as a teaching opportunity. Remember, delegating is about taking responsibility to ensure that the highest-value work gets done at the right levels. It is about pulling your people up and making them more capable.

This involves teaching. If you hesitate to delegate because it doesn't come out right, you need to find a better way to share with people what "right" looks like.

It is important not to take for granted what you know. Share the secret. One reason it comes out better when you do it is that you know what you really want. Think about how to share the process you go through. Communicate how you would assess the task or evaluate the quality of the deliverable. Provide clear descriptions of desired outcomes.

A great way to teach while delegating is to create templates or give examples for what it looks like when it's finished: "For this to work, it needs these eight components. The level of quality for each component is defined by. . . . It also needs these five questions answered."

Another great approach is to build in third-party checkpoints along the way. For example, instead of you being the one to review the quality for a product support plan, make one of the milestones review and approval by three salespeople, one in each region. That gives you a way to let your people really learn what "good enough" means for themselves. They are growing and will know better next time. You've done your job of getting the deliverable produced—and in the process you have also done your job of teaching and growing the capability of your team members.

Never Go in Alone

OK, sometimes you do need to jump in—in a crisis or if someone leaves unexpectedly. All kinds of things can occur that leave you no other choice in the moment than to jump in and do the work personally.

But here's something really important to remember: when you do need to jump in, never go in alone. Have someone on your team connected with the work in there with you, and make sure you use it as a teaching opportunity. Educate someone along the way, or you will be stuck again next time.

Be Unavailable

This technique actually works really well. Simply be unavailable. Stop coming to the rescue. If you have given your team training and support, and if you've created the right processes and checkpoints, if they know you are not available, they will deal with it.

Your team will survive; they will step up and deliver. If you are always available, though, you will always get sucked in.

Try this—really. You'll be pleasantly surprised.

Accept Imperfection

This might be the hardest thing to do, but it is fundamental to effective delegating and growing your team.

Let your team do the work and accept that it is not perfect, not as good as you would have done it. If it meets the defined desired outcome but it is not exactly as you would have done it, accept it as good enough and then encourage them to get feedback from others. They will learn how they can make it better, just as you did.

If you always nitpick and change everything your team does to be exactly the way you would do it, you are shooting yourself in the foot for the long term.

You may be more comfortable with the deliverables, but you are completely cutting off the possibility that, with your encouragement and support, they could become *even better at it than you*. In fact, you are limiting them to never being any better at it than you.

KEY INSIGHT: *If you prevent your people from getting better than you are at their tasks, you are failing as a leader.*

The whole point is to have everyone step up their skills. If you overmanage people, they will not be motivated to excel; they will just be motivated to get you off their back. In the long run you are failing to grow capacity and leaders at the levels beneath you.

Showing people that you trust them to do well is very powerful and encouraging. And part of that is accepting imperfection where it really doesn't matter. By doing this, you create the necessary environment for people to really grow.

Let People Fail

If you never let people fail, they never learn. If they fail, they will feel bad, get embarrassed, and have a strong personal need and drive to recover and excel—and then they will really learn what they need to do—just like you did.

Don't take that learning experience away from your people by always saving them from failure. It's important not only to delegate work but also to delegate decisions. If you never let people make and own some of the decisions, along with the associated outcomes, they will never be ready to step up to your level.

Change the Team

What if your team members just aren't capable of delivering good enough work? What if, after all the clearly defined outcomes and teaching and encouragement and support, they are still not able to step up and do the job you need?

So often managers seem to think that their job is to do the best they can with the team they inherited or that they have very nice and loyal people on the team, so it would be wrong to let them go.

Remember, it is your job to build and lead a team capable of doing excellent work, one that can step up to be even more capable over time. If you have tried to teach them and they are still not capable of stepping up, it is your job to replace them.

> **KEY INSIGHT:** *Standout leadership is not just accepting the team you inherited; it is building a team capable of working at a higher level. There is really no gray area here.*

You need to realize that you are expected to upgrade your team over time. The most competent leaders deal with low performers and build a team that is capable of doing the team's work, freeing themselves up to succeed at their more strategic, higher-level work. They redefine their job to add more value *while* rebuilding their team to be more capable.

Build *Your* Team

Whether you build a team from scratch or inherit a team, you must build a team that is capable of being delegated to. That means that your team must complement your strengths and fill in the gaps for your weak spots.

> **KEY INSIGHT:** *Your high-performing team would not necessarily be a high-performing team for a different leader who has different natural strengths and experience gaps. Every time you step into a role as a leader, you need to build your team.*

In my case, I always made sure that I had on my team a strong technology visionary, a strong financial manager, and a strong process support person.

Delegate to a Process

No matter what your role, think of your job as taking low-value, repetitive, reactive work out of the system by building systems and processes to make room for high-value work. Think about which activities suck up most of your time and create a process to streamline them.

If you can't delegate to a person, you can delegate to a process. You can always invent systems and processes to streamline and offload time-consuming activities. This frees up time for higher-value work.

If you are fielding "issue" phone calls 24/7, going to infinite review meetings, dealing with swarms of tasks as they land in your inbox, stand back and say, "Life can be better than this." *Stop* reacting. Understand what is repetitive and build a process.

Early in my career I was a product manager. I covered all aspects of product management and product marketing for my product line. I did not have a team. It was just me. One of the big time drains in my job was constantly responding to crises and questions from the field sales force. It would have taken up all of my time if I had let it.

So I came up with a process called "Gold Sheets." This was actually a paper-based process, before the Internet, so I feel like a dinosaur telling this story, but it is a great example of how much time you can save if you delegate to a process. I collected all the crises and questions from sales, sorted and grouped them, and wrote up the answers on a Gold Sheet. I sent it out in a "Gold Sheet Binder" that had tabs for Product News, Customer References, and Competitive Information. Every time something happened in the product line that I thought would be useful or important for the field to know, I wrote up a Gold Sheet on it and sent it out—probably two per week on average.*

Because this sales information came on a different color paper then the rest of the mail, it stood out. And because I had given my people a place to file the information, it didn't get lost. The sales force started carrying around their Gold Sheet binders because it helped them sell.

---

*Today I would use a blog to do this. As a product manager, I would have a sales support blog where I would regularly post updates and news to help sell the product. The great part is that sales reps could also share their experiences about what worked and didn't, so they could also learn in the moment from each other's best practices.

This Gold Sheet process reduced my onslaught of emergencies from the field by 90 percent. I freed up my time to work on other things.

I still remember the sales meeting where a sales rep started yelling at me for not delivering a promised work-around for a missing competitive feature. Before I could even start responding, the rest of the team whipped out their Gold Sheet binders and said, "Patty sent that out last week; you should have dealt with that already!"

KEY INSIGHT: *If you can create systems and processes to work more efficiently and effectively, you'll not only get the work done, but you'll also be seen as a leader who can prioritize, rise above the tactics, and build value in the business, rather than a known workhorse who can personally handle a virtually unlimited amount of work.*

* * *

The Hard (and Important) Part

Delegating *is* actually harder and slower in the moment than just doing the work yourself. And you remain responsible for the business outcome even if your employee screws it up. So it's just easier to keep control. That's all true.

But the reality is, you can pay now or you can pay later. If you invest now in teaching, in getting clear outcomes and measures defined, and in building confidence through trials and risks, then yes, it takes more time now, but it pays big dividends in the future.

If instead you take the shortest, easiest path and do stuff yourself because you can do it well and quickly, you will pay later. Your organization will not grow, and your effectiveness will degrade over time as the business gets harder, you get busier and busier, and you have failed to build a team who can step up. You have more important things to do than cover for a low-performing team.

Next . . . How the best leaders always raise the bar

8. Better with Less

Raise the Bar or Fall Behind

Don't get attached to the way you did things last time.

It's your job to figure out how to raise the bar—how to get the right stuff done better and more efficiently. The best leaders find ways to make their resources go further, as a general way of doing business.

Any smart person can do more good stuff with more money. But what happens if you get less money?

If you walk around saying "I can't do as much as I did last year because I don't have as much budget as I did last year," that's the wrong answer. This is another one of those puzzles that makes the most effective leaders stand out. They don't get stuck when this happens. Instead of trying to muscle through it the same way they did it last time but with less resources, they figure out a better way forward.

Do Great Stuff

High performers do great stuff no matter what their budget. It's a mix of Ruthless Priorities and finding ways to do *Better* with *Less*. Better doesn't need to mean *more*. Better often means different, smaller, more targeted.

When you focus on doing Better with Less, you are not squeezing, cutting, and degrading quality. You are challenging yourself and your team to invent a radical, new, and better way of doing things.

This is one of the most useful tools in your quest to deliver standout results. It is also a critical precursor to the next section, LOOK Better, because this particular way of working goes a long way toward growing your credibility along with your business impact.

For example, let's say you're marketing a new product. If you spend $1,000 on demand generation and it gets you 100 leads, there is a tendency to think that if you want to get 200 leads you need to spend $2,000. When you apply the Better-with-Less thinking, think about all the other things you could do to get 200 leads without spending a cent more. Make the program better. Make the copy more engaging to read. Make what you offer better, make the call to action easier, make the landing page more convenient and compelling, make the follow-up more focused, make the product better! If you challenge your team first to reinvent how you do something to get a better outcome and then budget it later, you will often find you can get a better outcome for less money because you have done the strategic thinking. You have invented a better way to do it.

Let's take another example. Say you are supporting a product and you need to support more customers next year. The tendency would be to increase the budget to support the larger customer base. Instead, have a discussion with your team about things you can do to provide better service to the customers you have now with the team you have now. Maybe make your online interface more useful and clear or add a community where users can support each other. Improve the support processes to route issues more quickly. Then when you get a new budget, you can apply it to creating a competitive advantage with your service, not just to funding an increase in capacity to do exactly the same thing.

Here are some ideas to focus how you work on the right things by taking the Better-with-Less approach.

Don't Get Hung Up on How Much Things Cost Last Time

We tend to think about budgets in terms of needing the same money for the same stuff we did last year plus new budget amounts for new stuff. If you get stuck in your way of thinking about what things cost, because they cost that last time, and build your plan on that cost, you run a big risk. What if you get *less* budget than last year? With this approach, your only option is to *do less*.

Now I want to be clear that I am not talking about doing *more* with *less*. That simply doesn't work, not to mention that everyone will roll their eyes and laugh at you behind your back when they hear it. And it is never a formula for success to pile more and more work on the same people with the same or smaller budget.

What I'm actually talking about is doing *less* with *less*, but in a way that makes the impact of what you do *better*. I remember one time my mantra was "We are going to be doing *less* with *less*, but it's going to be good!" People can buy into that.

You Own the Budget—Act Like It

Most leaders don't think about cutting their own budgets unless they are forced to do so. Here is where great leaders step up, on their own, because there is great value in doing so without being asked. I'm not suggesting you give the money back! But cutting your own budget gives you the power to free up resources to do new and better things.

> **KEY INSIGHT:** *If you never make room in your own budget to do new things, you and your team will be at risk because you will be viewed as doing things the old way as the business changes and grows.*

Here's how you can do this. Start by assuming you have the same budget as last year; then assign only 80 percent of it to your team. Force them to be creative about how they can deliver their part for less. Work as a team on the Better-with-Less scenarios.

Then present the 20 percent you held back as your fund for doing new, exciting, strategic stuff. That is so much more motivating than telling your team you can't afford the exciting new stuff because you are not getting any more money, and it is exactly what the business needs and expects you to do as a leader.

Be the New Guy Each Year

When you start a new job, you almost always see ways that the last guy was wasting time and money and not being as effective as you will be. So you be the new guy. Step into your own job anew, find all the stupid stuff you are doing, and improve it.

This is a great exercise to do with your team. Tell your team, "Let's list the stupid stuff we are doing." You will get a rousing discussion and a lot of ideas for things you can stop and improve. Make sure you do this at least once a year. Go through your key programs and brainstorm on the stupid stuff you should stop doing and how you can improve so you can deliver a better result with less work or less money. You'll be surprised at how many ideas you can come up with that don't cost anything.

Reduce Baseline Costs Year over Year

As a leader it is your job to cut the cost of doing the same stuff year over year—full stop.

Even if you get more money, wouldn't you rather spend it on higher-value stuff than let it go to maintenance activities?

This is a key practice that makes the most successful executives stand out, builds trust with your management, and puts you in the running for a bigger job. If you always ask for more money to do new stuff, you will be seen as less strategic and less competent. And more important, this key practice gives you the control to do new or more strategic stuff whether or not you get more money.

This is a big factor in building your credibility. You are showing that you can think like a businessperson, growing your part of the business and the capability of your organization, without always spending more money.

Real executives take cost out. Don't miss this. Just as you shouldn't accept your job description (as it is) as a life sentence, you shouldn't accept that things always need to cost as much as they did last year. You need to upgrade how your team delivers—it's expected of you as a leader.

* * *

The Hard (and Important) Part

Dealing with shrinking budgets and increased responsibility is a way of life. As a leader you can't let that prevent you from raising the bar and driving higher-value business outcomes each year. No one will help you with this. Your team will get annoyed that they have less money to do the same stuff. It's up to you to lead.

Your choices are either to negotiate for more budget or to make room in the budget you *have* to do new, higher-value stuff. It is never a choice *not* to do higher-value stuff. Remember, you need to rise above the work—it's not the work that matters, it's the value of the outcomes you deliver. Find a way.

Not raising the bar is a path to failure over time. This is the reason that some leaders don't "scale" as companies grow. Scaling is about changing and reinventing the way you work as the company gets bigger, to do things in bigger, more efficient, higher-value ways. If you can't figure out how to step up each year, no matter what your budget, your company will bring in someone who can scale.

Next . . . Trust is a big lever. Use it on purpose.

9. Trust and Consequences

You Are Either Building or Destroying Trust; There Is No Neutral

Trust is a big lever. Leaving trust to chance is either leaving a huge asset untapped or leaving an infection spreading through your organization.

For something that seems like a "soft" business thing, trust has a hard return on investment, because it helps you go faster and get more done.

A high-trust environment is a fast, competitive environment. A low-trust environment is a slow, dysfunctional environment. From a practical point of view, lack of trust gives you hundreds more questions, issues, and action items to deal with. It's a huge hidden expense in your business.

The tricky thing about trust is that there really is no neutral. If you are not actively building it, it is slipping away. You can't do nothing and keep trust. You have to do *something*.

You Establish the Environment and the Culture

Remember, as a leader, you shape the environment (if you are working at the right level). There is great value in treating trust-building as a concrete deliverable in your action plan.

So What Does Trust Help With?

If you step back and think about what happens when you have trust, you'll realize it's a lot!

If your employees trust you

- They will do more for you.

- They will go faster because they won't waste time wondering whether it is a good idea.

- They will spend less time worrying about their jobs.

- They will care. They will be more motivated.

- They will bring more energy and emotional commitment to their work.

If you trust your employees

- They will get more done for you, because being trusted is motivating.

- You will get more done for them, because they are worth it.

- They will use less of your physical, checking-in time or your mental time (spent worrying).

- They will grow into higher-performing employees.

If your boss trusts you

- You will spend less time explaining, defending, reporting, and changing gears.

If your peers trust you

- You will get more information, support, and help.

If your boss trusts your team

- You will be able to step up into bigger and better things because your boss will accept your team's stepping in for you.

If your boss's peers trust you

- You will have an advantage in budget and resource negotiations.

- You will be nearer to the head of the line for promotions.

If your boss's boss trusts you

- You can save your boss time and energy by stepping in.

- You can get more visibility and exposure in the process.

If your clients trust you

- They will buy more stuff.

- They will buy more quickly.

- They will recommend you to others.

Building and maintaining a high degree of trust is really worth it! Here are several ways to build trust with your organization on purpose.

Be *Yourself*: You Can't Fake Being You

Trust starts with being trustworthy.

When leaders are being true to themselves, it's really obvious—it can't be faked. Think about leaders and political figures you have seen. The ones who are being real people leap out from the crowd of their peers and competitors. They inspire people.

Being a whole person; sharing what you really care about, your values, your struggles; talking about things that actually mean something to you and why this business matters to you personally—all these things build trust.

On the other hand, leaders who are not showing up fully or not being authentic will destroy trust coming out of the gate.

Being Invisible and Absent

If you are not standing up as a leader, and not standing for anything in particular, then you are projecting apathy. If you are absent personally and emotionally, people will wonder why they should care or invest their time and emotional energy in the business. Leaders who don't stand for anything destroy trust.

The False Executive Persona

Leaders who stick to positioning, read from someone else's script, or manage themselves to be different from who they really are do not win trust. Whatever false persona you choose and whatever your motivations for doing so, just know that this destroys trust, because it is impossible to do it consistently. All you need to do is travel with an executive who is putting on a false persona and watch what happens when the flight get cancelled: the façade will crack and the real person will come out.

Being Inconsistent

Inconsistent personality is a big destroyer of trust. This goes back to the previous point. Be *you*. It's easier to maintain because you don't have to remember all the rules about how you are supposed to act. Be yourself. You will be much more consistent and build much more trust.

Don't Change Your Mind All the Time

Think about the last time you heard a new strategy from your executive management. What was your reaction? Likely there was a fair amount of skepticism about the strategy du jour. Or you might have been worried about the consequences of a change in strategy. Will you have a job? Will your job be the same? Or will it be different—and will you hate it?

These reactions come from too many changes in strategy or failure to communicate the strategy in a way that makes people believe they can trust you—or both. Each time you change your mind or your strategy, you destroy a little more trust.

The way to build trust is to select your Ruthless Priorities, as we discussed in chapter 2, and stick to them until they are finished. Then pick the next ones. Sticking to a strategy, actually getting stuff done, and actually making progress is a huge trust builder. People love to finish things.

Share What You Know

It is really easy to take for granted the things *you* see and do and experience and expect that everyone else also knows these things.

One of the biggest levers of trust I ever discovered was to put out a regular communication, every one to two weeks, about what I saw happening in the business. Deals won, projects completed, new hires, competitive moves, and, of course, reiterating the key priorities.

I discovered that the regular heartbeat of communications from someone at the top was even more important than the content of the message. It makes you very present as a leader. It builds a huge amount of trust. It also scores a disproportionate amount of leadership points compared to the effort.

This is useful—and not only if you have a large organization. Any organization that is more than just you has the problem of some people not knowing everything that other people know. As a leader, share what you know.

Hint: Share your regular updates with your peers and boss too. Your excellent updates will get forwarded around, and through your consistency, your sharing, and your presence as a leader, you will create huge amounts of trust.

If you are not sharing openly what you know, if people never hear any insights or thoughts from you about the business, and you don't take time to share what you are thinking, their confidence and trust in you will go down. Remember, there is no neutral.

Keep Communicating

We touched on this in chapter 2, Ruthless Priorities: the more you communicate, the more comfortable people will be with what you are saying. Consistent communication builds trust. Lack of communication or inconsistent communication destroys trust. Do it on purpose. Communicate more than you could ever imagine is necessary.

Caveat: Make sure your messages are clear, straightforward, and brief. Spending two hours to communicate one decision will bore and frustrate people. First be relevant, concise, and useful. Then repeat.

The weekly communication I did was a core part of my leadership approach, and it built a lot of trust with people because I kept it up. It became something that people could count on.

When times were difficult or uncertain, I didn't stop the communications. That was the point. The communications were always there. The consistency was the thing that built the most trust, not just the content.

Be Straightforward in Difficult Times

As a leader, the more straightforward you can be, the more trust you will build. You can't always tell your team everything. But you can do a lot to be as open as possible if you set that as your goal.

Make sure you talk in their language. Say, "You are probably worried about losing your job," not "Business conditions may cause challenging organizational pressures that might be of concern." The first builds trust; the latter degrades it.

Answer tough questions head on. Acknowledge when things are difficult. Give people a chance to talk about what they are worried about. Let them know that it is a difficult time and you are worried too, then reinforce your commitment to the business and talk about why you are staying there.

If you try to avoid all negative discussion or always put a positive spin on everything, you will be seen as clueless by your people who are experiencing the reality. That will destroy trust. If you acknowledge difficult issues, then get your team focused on what they can do during times of uncertainty, you will build trust.

Make the Work Matter

Humans work for more reasons than money—and money is not even at the top of the list. What is at or near the top of the list for people is to feel like their work matters, that it counts for something. This is a big trust issue. They are trusting you to make sure their work matters.

I heard an interview with Dan Ariely about his book *The Upside of Irrationality*. He talked about a test he did to measure how important meaning was in one's work. The test was to complete a task repeatedly until you wanted to stop. Paraphrasing the interview, the task was to build a LEGO robot. When you completed it, you got asked if you would like to build another robot. In one case the robot you built was placed to the side. In the other case, if you said you'd like to build another, they disassembled the one you just built right in front of you, gave you back the pieces and said, "OK, build another one."*

As I listened to the interview I thought, "That is one of the best metaphors I have ever heard for taking the meaning out of someone's work!"

It got me thinking about how we as leaders can drain meaning from our employees' work—we *disassemble their robots right before their eyes.* This is a huge trust issue! Why should they work so hard if it doesn't matter?

One of your most important tasks as a leader is to remove uncertainty. Uncertainty degrades trust. If your company is fuzzy about what its strategy is, it's really hard for people to understand whether their work matters or not. It is really demotivating for people to deliver work into a strategic black hole. It degrades trust.

It's like throwing their robots directly into the trash can.

Even if the strategy is clear to you, don't expect your staff to automatically see how their work fits into supporting the big picture. You need to spell it out and show them why their work matters. If you never connect the dots about how their work specifically supports the overall strategy, there is no meaning in it for them.

---

* Robert Siegel, "Exploring the Upside of Irrationality," interview with Dan Ariely, *All Things Considered*, NPR (June 1, 2010), http://www.npr.org/templates/story/story .php?storyId=127352130.

They are just putting their robots on a conveyor belt to be used for unknown purposes.

Ensuring that all your employees understand how the business works and how their work helps move it forward will build trust. It will motivate and enable them to make better decisions on behalf of the business and add more value themselves.

Hire Really Smart People

Leaders who are threatened by smart people, who therefore either avoid hiring them or lock them in supply cabinets, are destroying trust with everyone around them.

KEY INSIGHT: *One of the most important things you do as a leader is choose people.*

The smarter the people you choose, the more your whole organization will respect and trust you.

Let's look at the model in its purest form: if smart people hire only even smarter people, and those people hire only even smarter people, the organization gets even stronger and smarter as it grows. The leader is a hero and is highly trusted.

If stupid leaders who are threatened by smart people hire people less smart than they are, and so on, the entire organization gets more weak and stupid over time. The leader destroys all trust with high performers.

If you want to deliver remarkable results, you need to have as many remarkable people helping you as possible and to let them thrive and do amazing things for you.

KEY INSIGHT: *I have never seen a smart person damaged by letting a smarter person thrive beneath him or her.*

Letting really talented people shine is good for you, for them, and for the business. And it builds trust all around with everyone. If you are consistently generous with credit and give visibility to others where it is due, everyone will recognize that you are trustworthy.

Sadly, I have often seen managers who feel threatened by smart people and squash or limit them in an attempt to appear more qualified themselves. This destroys trust and keeps them from delivering at the level they need to. Ultimately, they lose the game and get moved out of the way.

Performance Management: Differentiate

If you stand by and look the other way when you have a poor performer on your team, you are squandering trust. Everybody sees it. If you think this is just between you and the low performer, think again. Everyone on the team sees what you are doing—and not doing—to manage performance, good or bad.

You must get comfortable with differentiating. Treating everyone equally is not fair to your high performers. If you treat your high performers the same way you treat your low performers, you will create several problems:

- Your high performers lose trust in you because their great work doesn't count for anything—"There are no consequences for slacking off, so why should I kill myself?"

- You let everyone know you are not serious about managing performance, so motivation of the whole team goes down.

- Your low performers get away with it, so your high performers do less work, so you deliver less.

- More trust degrades, because the capability of your team goes down, so you fail to deliver at the level you need to.

Building Trust with Individuals

All of my suggestions about building trust with your team also work to build trust with individuals, but there are a few more things you can do specifically to build trust with individuals.

Ask What to Worry About

Don't assume you know what you should be concerned about. Don't do unto others as they would do unto you. Do unto others as *they would like to have done unto them*. Don't guess—*ask*.

Do this now. With each of your reports, say the following: "As your manager I am going to worry about what matters to you. When I worry about you, what should I worry about?"

I guarantee you will be surprised and amazed by what you hear. We tend to think that everyone wants more money, promotions, stock options, recognition—you know, the usual stuff. But you will hear things you *never* would have guessed, let alone assumed.

Let me give you an example. I asked this question of a man who worked for me (in California). He got quiet for a minute and then said, "My father is dying. He is in Boston. I am worried that I won't get to spend time with him." My response: "You are as of now transferred to Boston. Report in when you get settled."

Never in a million years would I have known this if I hadn't asked. How easy was it to do something about it? I started that conversation worried about the fact that I couldn't give him a well-deserved raise. That didn't matter to him at all. I was able to do something that made a huge difference to him as a human. Trust is built on an individual level by being human, getting to know people as humans, and treating them like humans, not like "workers" or "resources."

Here are some other things I have heard: "I am worried about getting school set up for my child with a learning disability," or "You don't need to worry about me, but I'd like you to worry about this other guy." And I have had senior men and women start to cry when I asked, because no one in their entire career had ever asked what they care about.

I can't overemphasize the value of doing this.

Trust People to Learn and Deliver

In the previous chapter we talked about effective delegating. Trust is a huge issue in delegating. When you delegate something, you wonder, "Can I trust this person to deliver?" And the person thinks, "Will you trust me to deliver?" I can tell you that, particularly when delegating to high performers, trust is a very big motivator.

Think about it this way. If you pick apart everything your employee does and insist that it comes back looking exactly the way you would have done it, you have squandered a real opportunity. You've taken away the person's motivation to learn.

> **KEY INSIGHT:** *If you send people the signal that you trust them, and you encourage them to do big things, they will be more motivated to do big things. And more often than not, they will do them.*

One of my favorite stories about this happened when I worked at a software business. We hired a guy to help us sort our support contracts. We initially viewed this as mostly a sorting and filing job.

As he got into it, he realized that it was such a mess, he couldn't figure out what was happening without talking to customers. We wondered, "Should we trust him to talk to customers?" We decided to.

A week later, he came to me and said, "I have been talking to customers and getting these contracts sorted out. I am finding that some customers are behind on their support. Would you like me to sell them new support contracts?"

Another week later, he told us, "You know, while I have these customers on the phone talking about support, I ask them if they have more people who would benefit from our products than they have licenses for. Would it be OK if I sold them products too?"

If you hire smart people and show them you trust them, they will do amazing things for you.

It Gets Less Scary over Time

Letting people fail and learn and grow by trusting and supporting them also makes them trust you even more. Because of that, they will feel comfortable coming to you for help and guidance when they need it.

You get more comfortable too. You trust that they are doing their best and that if they run into difficulties, they will come to you. You trust them to not fail without signaling for help.

The result: You spend less time, get more work done, and develop someone in a really meaningful way.

Consequences Matter

If someone doesn't deliver, doesn't show up on time, or doesn't follow the rules, there must be consequences. Without consequences, there is no reason for people to believe what you say. If you say something is important, but then it doesn't happen and you do nothing about it, you are degrading trust.

We all have our own style, and we need to do what we're supposed to do in our own style. You don't end up firing people for every single thing that does not happen as planned. But it is imperative that you have a "What happened? This is unacceptable. What are you going to do about it?" conversation.

Although these are not fun, comfortable conversations, if you avoid them, you are degrading trust. People need to know that delivering matters. They need to see that you are consistently reinforcing the things you claim to care about.

Holding people accountable builds trust; looking the other way or waffling on what is important destroys it.

Tough on Expectations and Results but Kind to People

Clarity is very important here. You need to be very clear on outcomes, expectations, measures, and consequences. Then when something doesn't happen as it should, you have a nonpersonal way of showing it and discussing the gap. If you didn't complete the step of setting expectations clearly and you can have only a vague conversation to the effect that the result is not good enough, it too easily becomes a personal judgment. Clarity of expectations builds trust in itself because people know what to expect and what they will be measured and judged on.

So be clear and be really hard on the results, but treat the person with consideration and respect. Even when you are being tough on a failure to deliver, personally engaging with the person as a human builds trust for the future.

The Hard (and Important) Part

The hardest part about building trust is that you need to be unfailingly consistent. As soon as you let up, change your mind, disappear for a while, don't pounce on a consequence, let something slide, fail to give credit, or back off on communicating, you are degrading trust.

I have a mentor who describes this part of leadership as "the hard, boring, and required stuff." Stay ever diligent on measures, consequences, and communicating. The payoff is big.

Next . . . How to LOOK Better, build your
executive presence, communicate with the
people who matter, and stand out as a leader

Part 2

LOOK Better
Be Visible,
But Not Annoying

Good work doesn't stand on its own.
Build your credibility with the people
who can help you (or blacklist you).

10. Credibility and Relevance

Credibility Is Inversely Proportional to Obstacles

I've seen talented people really miss the boat here. Their work is outstanding. The outcomes they deliver are valuable to the business. Yet they are not recognized and respected. They feel invisible, unappreciated, and taken advantage of. I frequently hear people say, "Management doesn't value my input."

This is not the fault of management. The issue is credibility and relevance. To get your inputs viewed as valuable, you need to do the work to establish yourself. Then they will listen.

Why Credibility Matters

Without personal credibility, *everything* is harder, slower, and more frustrating. Everything is an uphill battle. You get a much lower return on your effort. You waste time, and you burn significant career capital, because you never get enough credit for what you contribute, and your opinions and inputs are not sought out or welcome.

Credibility gives you both a time advantage and a trust advantage. It helps you get more done, go faster, and avoid stupid questions and the need to endlessly defend your honor. It helps you attract top talent, money, and the best projects. Credibility makes you more effective.

I wish I had learned this much earlier in my career—building credibility should be a specific item on your task list. Good work does not stand on its own. Delivering results alone does not ensure you will get recognized and rewarded. It's sad but true. You need to take it upon yourself to make your work visible and make it count.

Credibility Is Not Just a Publicity Exercise

It's important to note that although good work doesn't stand on its own, *credibility does not happen without good results*. The last thing you want to do is go on a campaign to build your credibility if you don't deserve it! It all starts with exceptional results and *then* creating positive visibility for those results. LOOK Better builds on DO Better.

Some people are also concerned that this credibility exercise feels selfish because it's about getting attention for yourself. The fact of the matter is, the higher your personal credibility, the more useful and valuable you are to your projects, your team, and your company. It's not selfish because it's not just about you. It's about increasing your value to your projects, team, and business.

For example, in negotiating for resources, the executive with higher credibility will get the advantage every time. If you are trying to get around a corporate system to get a nonstandard raise approved for a team member, you will get nowhere without high credibility. If you need to get support from another organization, without high credibility you will be facing a brick wall.

Get More Done

Think about credibility as a critical enabler to getting anything significant done. I know a librarian in the Midwest who said that although she didn't work in a corporation, she realized that it was important to build her professional credibility so she could inspire donors and local politicians to keep the library funded. Credibility is both a powerful weapon and a shield. It helps you advance your cause and defend your progress.

Get Bigger Results

People with high credibility get more support. So they get more approvals, budget, and resources than everybody else. They are the ones who can go out on a limb, redefine, or add to their jobs to do bigger things. So they can deliver bigger outcomes. People with high credibility are given a bigger platform on which to build remarkable results.

Go Faster

Credibility is inversely proportional to roadblocks. People with high credibility get to spend less time defending their honor and their decisions. They can work faster, and they deal with fewer stupid questions like these: "Why are you spending money on that? Why did you hire this person? Wouldn't it be better if you did this?"

Here is an example of what I mean. I have a colleague who is a marketing executive in a cosmetics company. He spent a significant amount of time developing his marketing plan for the following year with the associated budget. It got approved. He was excited to move on to the more important work of actually doing the stuff in the plan, but he got blocked.

Peers started asking him questions. "Why are you spending so much on PR?" "Why aren't you investing more in Asia?" "Why are you doing social media instead of more events?" Even though his plan had been approved, he ended up in defensive mode. He had to attend meeting after meeting to explain and justify his plan. He was forced to prepare yet another, special presentation, just to explain the budget and "sell" his plans again. It took a lot of time, but he was stuck doing it. He couldn't move forward on the work until he addressed the latest round of stupid questions and got approval—again.

This process almost never adds value to either your plans or the business, but it's an activity that happens over and over again—except for the leaders who have high credibility.

Having high credibility gets you a pass. People with high credibility are given the benefit of the doubt because their judgment is generally trusted. You may still be asked to take a budget cut from time to time, but you won't be asked to defend your honor over and over again.

People with high credibility have great teams.

Great people respond to, gravitate to, and stay working for leaders with high credibility. People who can attract top talent and motivate them have the horsepower to create more success than everyone else.

Once you think about credibility as a goal unto itself, you can start building and maintaining it on purpose. Here's how.

Be Relevant to the Business

The most important factor in building your credibility is to make sure that your work is highly relevant to the business. It's up to you to connect the dots between what you do and what matters to the business.

Remember, it's always about the business outcomes, not the work. You always need to ask, what successful business outcome did my work create or enable? Did my work bring in new revenue? Did it take cost out? Did it find a new market? Did it close a competitive gap? Did it help us go faster? Did it build a team capable of winning or enabling new business? Did it create a product or service that customers love and pay for?

Think Like a General Manager

General managers care about business outcomes. To connect your work to relevant business outcomes, always be asking, "What are the overall business outcomes that matter most right now?" And always be thinking, "How does my work enable or drive those outcomes?"

Invest the time to understand what the CEO is worrying and talking about. What are the key initiatives in the business? What markets are top priority? What is needed to go after them? What is the CEO most focused on inventing or changing? What operating efficiencies are being targeted? What customer initiatives are critical right now?

No matter what level you are at in the organization, if you put the business outcomes at the center of your thinking and discussions, you will find ways to associate your value with top-of-mind, high-value business outcomes. You will be building credibility because you are being relevant to the business.

Don't Try to Educate People
about Your Function

KEY INSIGHT: *If you need to educate people about what you do, by definition, you are not relevant.*

Just think about that for a moment. You want to be able to walk into a room of decision makers and have their attention and support because you are talking about something they understand and care about. If you need to educate them first, then by definition, it's not relevant, because they don't *already* understand and care about it.

You are digging yourself out of a credibility hole before you even get started.

Be a Translator

Here is the way to bridge the gap between what you do and what they care about: *To be relevant, you need to be a translator when you communicate with people outside your function.* I refer to this as using your "outside voice."

Your "inside voice" is the voice you use with your team, within your functional area. It has all your jargon and all your internal measures and priorities. It's all about describing and measuring what is important to *you*.

Your "outside voice" is your general manager voice, your business voice. It's the voice that is relevant to the people outside your function. It's about business initiatives, not functional projects.

For example: If you are trying to educate an executive team or a business unit manager about your brand campaign or data center investment or vertical market program, remember that those things are not relevant to them. Only their business initiatives are relevant to them. Trying to show and explain the value of what you are doing in your terms will waste time and annoy you and them. Instead, learn about their business and translate everything you say into *their* vocabulary.

Here are some examples:

- Your multiquarter integrated marketing campaign becomes "Help increase the size of deals for these three product lines and move them to close more quickly."

- Your IT data center investment to upgrade systems and software becomes "Improve information flow with our partners to increase inventory turns."

Here's how to do this. Interview your business stakeholders about their business. What business drivers are they most focused on? What initiatives do they see as most critical? What issues are they most concerned about?

You are listening for two things:

1. The list of things they care about

2. The exact words they use to describe them

They are giving you the specific content and vocabulary you need to be relevant in terms of what they care about.

Here is the big idea: The next time you talk to them about anything, prepare your discussion or proposal by "replaying the tape"—only use their words.

Organize your ideas, proposals, and initiatives with labels and headings that comprise only *their words* describing *their initiatives*. Use this technique to develop your "outside voice." Then, when you talk about your work, they will be associating you and your work with the things they already want and care about.

Always keep your functional jargon for your "inside voice" within your function, and always translate and use your "outside voice" when you communicate outside your function. Create support for your team and your work by using terms the business can relate to, understand, and appreciate. Otherwise you are just talking and getting mostly ignored or dismissed—not actually getting any visibility, appreciation, recognition, or support.

Credibility and Budget Discussions

You probably think of your budget in terms of planning and operational management. That's what it's for, of course. (Think "inside voice" for this aspect of your budget.) But it's very important to realize that presenting your budget to approvers and stakeholders is also a critical *communication* task, one in which you must not only communicate but also persuade people outside your function.

> **KEY INSIGHT:** *If there ever was a time to use your "outside voice," it's to present your budget. It puts you in the position of asking for money to pay for things your approvers really care about and want. If you use your "inside voice," you are just giving them a list of expensive functional jargon the value of which they don't understand.*

So you must see the act of presenting your budget as a key opportunity to build your credibility *and* get the money! Once you have high credibility, budget conversations are much easier because you get the benefit of the doubt.

It goes back to thinking like a general manager. If you always talk to executive management only about your function—if you only ever advocate about your plans, your budget, and your functional objectives—you are not thinking like a general manager. You are only using your "inside voice." You are demonstrating that you only understand and care about your own world and your own function. This is not building credibility.

So many times during the budget discussion, with the best of intentions, we set our sights on getting the biggest budget possible for our team or function so that we can deliver the most value with it. But strident advocacy for your function in the absence of a larger business context can degrade your credibility. You need to show that you can think like a general manager about the whole business and put the business first, at the center of your thinking and discussions.

If you are always seen as asking for more money to execute your team's function, you will not be as credible as if you step back, understand what is going on across the business, and demonstrate ways to be more efficient, cut costs, or even give some money back to support something more critical. Step above the work. You can build credibility by getting famous internally for being business minded and for personally helping with brilliant and creative cost management that doesn't sacrifice value.

As we discussed in chapter 8, Better with Less, it is critical for any leader to reduce the cost of doing the same things year over year. If you ask for the same budget as last year to do all the steady-state stuff and then you need incremental budget to do new stuff every year, your credibility will degrade. You need to self-fund some of the new stuff by reducing the cost of maintaining your current programs. No one should need to tell you to do this.

Do Your Job *and* Do More

I have spoken with many talented people who are surprised to learn that consistently doing excellent work and flawlessly delivering on their job description does not make them a top-ranked employee.

Doing your job well, as defined, keeps you from getting fired. What makes you stand out is finding additional ways to add value to the business over and above what is in your job description. Otherwise, you are just one more person doing what is expected of them.

Generate Revenue

Nothing will make you stand out more than having a direct effect on revenue. For an executive, taking on a troubled sales region and turning it around, or shoring up a struggling product line so it becomes profitable and is growing, are good paths to big career gains.

Not everyone is in a position to do something at this level, but don't be too quick to assume you are not in a position to affect revenue. Here are just a few ideas:

- Going on a customer visit and realizing that you could make a small change to an existing product to create a new product and revenue stream for a new segment

- Doing customer support and finding a recurring new service opportunity

- Being the one to search Twitter for discussions of your company's products, then turning unhappy customers into loyal purchasers

- Implementing a system that helps sales reps close more business

Associating your work with the bottom line builds huge credibility.

Improve Productivity

Every year you should have one explicit goal to improve productivity in your team (and in yourself). Your team should be more capable next year than this year. Some ideas: have better meetings, make project review processes more efficient, build a process for handling chaotic ad-hoc work, implement a better measurement and accountability framework, use the Web for better employee communication. . . . The list is endless.

You should always be working on at least one productivity improvement for yourself and in your team. See also chapter 6, The Level Dilemma. Being recognized for improving efficiency builds your credibility.

Be the Voice from Outside the Company

You must keep educating yourself, watching for examples of how others do things, and learning from customers. Bringing the external voice of the real world back into your business sets you up as highly credible because most people don't bother.

But make sure there is a point to it. It's not just about sounding smart. It's not about being that frustrating person who talks about all the stuff going on in the market but uses it to show why "that won't work" or has no action to propose. It's about bringing high-value, real-world input into the business to cause positive action and drive meaningful outcomes.

Develop Talent

It is critical for managers to be on the lookout for talent and to develop leaders below them in the organization. The best leaders I know take this on as almost a personal quest. They view it as an ongoing, primary responsibility. No one asks them to do this. They are always on the lookout for ambitious, high-potential people, and they make it a point to help them grow.

Developing talent is truly standout leadership behavior. I have interviewed hundreds of people for management and executive positions. The number of candidates who proactively talked about developing people without being asked was about five. They really stood out! Being known as a developer of people gives you a huge credibility advantage.

Innovate

We tend to think of innovation as only inventing a new product or getting a patent on a new idea (that can be turned into a product). Why limit innovation? For starters, innovation absolutely applies to what we just talked about: generating revenue, improving productivity, developing talent, and communicating.

Innovation should occur in all aspects of the business. Here are some places I think businesses have opportunities to innovate: how you interact with customers, how you manage business processes with partners, how you deal with IT service issues, how you evaluate the competition, how you use social media, how you bundle and price, how you reuse information.... Don't leave innovation to "the lab." Understand your business at the grassroots level and look for ways to make an impact.

The Hard (and Important) Part

Building credibility feels like extra work that you shouldn't need to do. You may resent it. After all, results should stand on their own. But your results will get lost and your career will stall if you don't do things on purpose to build your credibility.

Make sure your hard work is recognized. You need to be the one to demonstrate why your results matter and how valuable they are to the business. Connect the dots for people. *Make sure the points actually make it onto the scoreboard.* Otherwise your hard work will just be absorbed and largely unappreciated by your company, and you will continue to waste precious time defending your decisions, resources, and career.

Next . . . What are you known for? Is it what you want?

11. Your Personal Brand

You Have a Personal Brand, Whether You Know It or Not;
Is It What You Want?

How do people describe you to others when you are not there? I know that as a new leader, I was surprised to find out that people talked about me at all! Then I was surprised by what they were saying.

People, right now, have a specific impression of you.

Do you know what they think? Is it positive or negative? Or are you mostly invisible?

Do you know specifically what you are doing to give people the impression they have of you?

Many people want to improve how they position themselves in their company and how they appear to peers and stakeholders outside their company. They feel like they are not getting the recognition, credit, or respect they deserve.

What do you want to be known for? Is there a gap? How can you tip the scales in your favor?

Having a strong personal brand is critical to building your credibility and putting your best foot forward in a consistent way. It ensures that people know you for what you want to be known for. Don't leave it to chance. Manage it.

Brand Misunderstanding

Before we talk about personal brand, I want to talk about what *brand* really means. Brand is one of the most misunderstood concepts in business.

At a company level, many people think brand is about your logo or the colors on your website or your television commercials. Many people believe brand is a marketing job.

Brand is more fundamental than that. Whether you are a company or an individual, brand is about what you stand for and how you behave, not what you say.

You cannot tell the world what your brand is. (Well, strictly speaking, you can tell them anything you want—you just can't expect them to believe it!)

Your customers grant your company's brand to you based on the things they consistently experience from the products, employees, communications, and policies of the company. To explain this, a ready example is Disney. Disney has a very strong brand of being "the happiest place on earth." But it's not because some marketing person said so. Disney builds "happiest place on earth" into all their operations. They have done extensive research to reduce wait times. They have processes for reuniting children who get lost at the park with their families. They put the place where you pay the huge entry fee really far away from the fun stuff. They have strict rules and a code of behavior for their park employees (whom they call performers). They make it a point from the ground up to ensure your perception is that every Disney theme park is the happiest place on earth. However, if you went to Disneyland and got pissed off around every corner, it would not have a brand of being the happiest place on earth, no matter what marketing said.

Just as a corporate brand is defined by customers' experience with the company, your personal brand is defined by people's experience with *you*. Your personal brand is defined and granted to you by others, based on how they perceive their experience with you over time. So you have a personal brand today, whether you know it or not!

Behaviors and Consistency

If you take away only two ideas about brand, here's what they should be:

1. Behaviors

2. Consistency

Because your brand is conveyed by your behaviors, it is formed by the things that you do consistently. Do you do anything consistently? Do you do anything on purpose to give people a particular impression of you? What are you putting out there? Is it working for you?

Being Good Doesn't Help If You Are Inconsistent

I once went into a shop in California when I had some time to kill. I had about an hour between meetings, and this was a women's clothing shop that looked fun but was not anywhere near my style of dressing. It kind of looked like a place where belly dancers would shop! I was welcomed warmly (in my black business suit) by the shop owner, and she persuaded me to try on all kinds of crazy outfits. It was fun (there are no photos). I actually bought a few things.

The brand values I assigned to this shop owner, based on my experience, were *fun*, *personal*, and *successful experience*.

Several months later, I went to the same store on purpose, hoping for a similar experience. The owner wasn't there, but I had a remarkably similar experience to the first time. The woman in the shop focused lots of personal attention on me and on another customer as well. She got us interested in one another. I tried on lots of stuff and ended up, again, having fun and buying something.

I left the store that time thinking, "These people are managing their brand on purpose!" Two different people, several months apart, and the same *fun*, *personal*, and *successful experience*. I was very impressed with the care they were taking to convey their brand through their consistent behaviors.

A few months later I went to the store a third time, now fully expecting my *personal, fun, successful* brand experience (which is kind of why I went there at all—side note: a strong brand builds loyalty and support). In fact, I brought a friend this time, and the owner was there again.

But this time she was downright nasty. She could not have cared less about us. She was rushing us out of the store, and when I asked about the price of a small item she said, "I don't even know how much this costs; I usually give these away when someone makes a *real* purchase."

Yikes! Can you spot the brand letdown here? I've never gone back, but this story shows the power of consistency. When you let people know what to expect from you because you behave consistently, you build up credibility and trust with them. And if you break that consistency, you destroy trust, you lose credibility, and you dramatically weaken your brand.

Being inconsistently good just pisses people off. It creates a high expectation and then a big letdown. You have probably had experiences with people or businesses where you came to expect a particular level of service based on past experience and were then really let down when it was different.

KEY INSIGHT: *It's better to be consistently bad than inconsistently good!*

On the contrary, I have also seen people who have personality traits that are hard to take, people whom others don't like, but they are so consistent in their behaviors that they are trusted and respected.

There was one guy in the finance department in a Fortune 100 company who really had a foul personality. He was arrogant and disrespectful to anyone he came in contact with—and not just a little. Alas, he was being his real self. But he was also really good at his job. I don't think anyone really liked to spend time with this guy, but they knew they could always trust his advice, so they went to him. He was so unfailingly consistent in how he dealt with people that it came to be part of his brand. People always knew what to expect. They could brace themselves for it. I actually think it would have been much worse if he had tried to be nice sometimes, because he would not have been able to maintain it all the time. So then people would go in with their guard down and get really slammed.

I'm not recommending treating people badly, but in this case, his consistency helped him earn a lot of respect even though people didn't like him.

Developing Your Brand

Your personal brand will uniquely describe you. It will be based on who you really are, what you are naturally good at, and what you really care about. Your brand will incorporate your core strengths and values. It will be a description of your best self.

How would you describe your best self? What do you want to be known for? The answers define the foundation for your personal brand. Then, once you define what you want your brand to be, you need a strategy to behave that way on purpose. Your consistent behaviors will sell your brand to others.

Here is how you can build a strong personal brand that will be unique to you, help you be more effective, and make you stand out.

Your Current Brand

A good place to start is to get a baseline. What is your personal brand today? Find out what you are already known for. Get feedback.

Here are some questions you can use to get a picture of your current brand. Give these questions to five to fifteen people who know you. Get a broad perspective of present and past colleagues, friends, and family. (You will be surprised at how much your family knows about how you act at work.)

- When you observe me at work or life, what is always true? What do you always see?

- What is my manner of communicating?

- What do I "look like" when I am delivering?

- What am I expert in?

- How do I relate to others at work: What do I give? What do I expect?

- How do my personality and values affect what I offer?

- What outcomes do you associate with my being involved in something?

Define Your "Brand Attributes"

Next, add your own thoughts. Think about the things that define you, based on your strengths and your values. Think about your skills, competencies, and personality. Create a description of your best self.

- Make a list of the things you want to be known for. This can be a long list. This is the time to brainstorm. List all of your thoughts about who you are and what you do at your best.

- Compare and combine that list with what you learned from others' input.

- Highlight the things that make you most different from others.

- Sort the overall long list into categories or themes that define what you most want to be known for. (Aim for three to five at most.)

- These themes become your brand attributes.

Put the information about the brand attributes you created above in the *first column* on the worksheet on the opposite page.

Define Your "Brandable Behaviors"

The most important part of the brand-building exercise, and the element that will bring your brand to life, is to consider what behaviors will best showcase your brand. As you define each brand attribute, think of what you would specifically be doing, saying, offering, or creating to demonstrate that part of your brand. Think about what the video of you behaving that way would look like. Note those observable behaviors in the *second column*.

It's also worth thinking about the flipside. What alternate behaviors would degrade your brand? What things do you want to make sure *not* to do? Put those in the *third column*.

Things I want to be known for (brand attributes)	Behaviors that will reinforce my brand	Behaviors that will sabotage my brand

Here is an example. I worked with a guy who aspired to have a brand value of *worth listening to*. He wanted people to seek out his opinion and always be ready to listen when he had something to say.

So we worked through some specific things that would impact that brand value. Here is how this *worth listening to* brand attribute was built in the worksheet.

Things I want to be known for (brand attributes)	Behaviors that will reinforce my brand	Behaviors that will sabotage my brand
Worth listening to	Send very few emails. Never use "Reply all." Send emails only to people who need to know or act on what I am saying.	Emails that are too long and have the point of action buried at the end
	Speak in meetings only when my discussion has a specific, actionable impact on the subject at hand.	Talking in meetings to sound smart about things that have no impact on the business or action associated with them
	Go out of my way to frame thoughts in the vocabulary and context of my listeners. Make *sure* what I say is immediately relevant.	Talking in my own technical vocabulary and expecting people to make an extra effort to understand what I am saying

Be Unique

Another important point to note about brand is that even if you do everything brilliantly, if there are no consistent behaviors that people see all the time, your brand will be a blank. If someone is asked to describe you, they won't have much to say. You won't stand out. If you want to be recognized, you need to be recognized for something in particular.

So as you develop your brand attributes, look for the traits that make you uniquely you. Think about how you do things differently from others. Create a description of your best self that reflects who you really are in a way that shows how you are different and valuable.

Work with a Partner

It is very helpful to work with a partner on this brand-building exercise. These thoughts are much easier to access when you are talking about it with someone who can ask you questions, help pull all these things out of you, and remind you what is special. Our unique traits that make us most valuable are sometimes the things we can't see in ourselves.

Meet a few times with your partner, every one to two months, and help each other define and document your personal brand attributes. Go out into the world and try your brand on. Tune your definition and your behaviors as you learn and get reactions from people.

How Do You Know When You Are Done?

You will know you are finished defining your brand when it is useful to you—when it's not just a list of things in a file somewhere. When your brand is at the top of your mind all the time, and it's informing you how to act on a day-to-day basis, then you've got it.

KEY INSIGHT: *Once you define your brand, you can tune what you do—every single day; in every single meeting; in every single memo, email, or presentation; and in every single conversation—to support your brand.*

Changing or Improving Your Brand

Many people ask me: "Can I change what my brand is?"

Absolutely: You can modify the brand attributes you select to be something you aspire to—something that isn't quite true yet, or if it is true, that people don't yet recognize you for. Doing some thinking and definition work up front on what you want your new brand to be will help you tune your behaviors consistently to convey a new, improved impression of you.

For example, my husband is really smart. He had a brand value of being *smart*. Although he was indeed really smart, he didn't like the word "smart" because it seemed too boring to him. (This is a man who quit Mensa because they wouldn't have barbeques.)

So to begin with, we changed the brand label from *smart* to *clever*, because *clever* seemed less boring. But he still wanted to change his brand even more. He was starting a new job as a CIO and wanted to make sure that he was known not just for being clever, but also for being someone who takes decisive action on things.

So we created a brand attribute for him: *applied clever*. And this label served as a reminder for him that in every single meeting and interaction, if he was in danger of saying something clever, he was going to partner that with an action statement: "This very clever thing I just said implies that we will DO this specific thing, and the first step is to DO this part immediately."

If you want to change your brand from what it is today, it's great if you have an aspirational gap—something you want to strive for. But be careful not to define a gap so big that you can never fill it. If you create too big a gap, it will never become your real brand, because you could never live up to it consistently.

Your Brand Makes You More Effective in Your Work

Once when I was doing some marketing for my business, I was working with a system that had various templates for things to automate email communications with my clients. I was working on a pair of templates that were being used to respond to customer subscriptions to a monthly article from my website (pre-blog).

The first template was the "Thank you for your subscription" message.

The second template was where the current article would be attached.

I must have spent ninety minutes trying to type the first message. Thank you for your subscription, and so on. . . . I could not write a two-sentence email that I was happy with.

My husband came in and asked me how I was doing. When I told him about my struggle, he said, "Don't you have a brand value of *straightforward*? Wouldn't a straightforward person just send the thing the person asked for? Why are you sending a second, extra message? Just send them the thing they asked for." (Now that's Applied Clever!)

Indeed, that is what a straightforward person would do. That is why I was struggling so much with this "extra" message. The mere existence of the message contradicted my brand value of *straightforward*.

If you have your brand defined, you can use it as a filter or a guidebook for everything you do.

Your Brand Helps You Sell Yourself

Many people wish they could position themselves in their best light more of the time. We all have those moments of brilliance when we do a presentation, a negotiation, or a sales call and walk away thinking, "Man, I was great! I would buy that!"

Having your personal brand defined lets you be that impressive version of yourself on purpose all the time instead of being surprised when it occasionally happens!

Here is a great example of a woman who used her personal brand to sell herself. She was a forty-something consultant who found herself bidding for work in an Internet startup company full of twenty-something hipsters. She was initially concerned that she would not fit with their culture—like she might be viewed as their mother! She was concerned she would be undervalued and they wouldn't want to work with her. But because she had her personal brand defined, she decided not to worry about it. Instead she went in unapologetically, showing her brand—which was about focus, achieving clarity, and translating ideas into revenue.

Staying on brand made it easy for her to engage this group. It removed the stress and the uncertainty of the meeting. By focusing on her brand, she gave herself the opportunity to sell her strengths without hesitation.

Instead of being cautious and defensive and trying to earn their respect and sell her value on their terms, she wowed them on her terms. She got the job.

Your Brand Gives You Confidence

Because you build your brand based on who you really are, on your real strengths and values, your brand not only helps you be consistent but also allows you to act in a way in which you are naturally strong and comfortable. And that gives you confidence. Once you have confidence, you are better at everything!

We are all faced with difficult situations and decisions regularly in our careers. What should we do about the angry customer? How should we trade off investments? Who should we give our time to? How should we communicate bad news?

If you have your brand defined, you can be much more decisive and clear minded as a leader, just like the woman in the previous example who won the job. You can always refer to your brand and ask yourself, "What would a person like that do?" You give yourself the gift of confidence.

For example, parts of my personal brand are to be *straightforward, useful,* and *fair.* If I had to shut down a business unit or negotiate a new partnership, I found it very helpful to be able to go to my brand for advice. What would a straightforward, useful, and fair person do in this situation?

I would make sure to use very *straightforward* language in meetings where people were concerned about losing their job; I would say things like, "I'm sure you are concerned about losing your job." I would give them as much *useful* information as possible, like schedules for when we would know answers to things we did not know yet, and I made sure that whatever deal was struck was as *fair* and respectful to the individuals as possible. Having my brand clear in difficult leadership situations helped me feel confident in what I was doing and how I was doing it.

Have One Brand for Work and Life

So many people ask me if they should have a brand for who they are at work and a different brand for who they are outside of work. The most common version of this is that people feel like they have a nonwork brand, based on who they *really* are, that is just not appropriate for work.

I spoke with one woman who was a surfer. She was very relaxed on the weekends, and her friends saw her as warm, funny, fun. She told me, "I could never be that person at work. I would lose all respect. I need a work brand that is more serious, driven, and focused."

I said, "No. The more you split your work and life personalities, the more unsatisfying your life will be. It will be more painful to go to work in the morning, and you will be less effective at work because you are wasting energy on being someone else."

Why not align with natural strengths and who you really are instead? If your work brand is contrived and not based on who you actually are, you will not be as strong a leader. You will not build trust because by not being yourself, you are not being authentic. And it will be really hard to behave consistently because you are setting yourself up to try to behave in a way that is not really you. You are bound to slip up.

Why not take the surfer to work?

Maybe a merged work-life brand could start with warm, caring, and funny, and turn into something like this:

Brand Attribute: Engaged with people
At home: Warm, caring
At work: Connected, gets lots of input, respectful

Brand Attribute: Fast thinker
At home: Funny
At work: Quick wit, articulate, creative

Think about the things that are always true about you and how you can tune the behaviors that support those things for both work and life.

What about the Margaritas?

I'm not suggesting that you need to behave exactly the same way at work and on the weekends, showing up at the office in your beach clothes. But you can certainly still be the same person who enjoys surfing and margaritas when you go to work.

I know in my case when I stopped trying to pretend that I was more businesslike and serious (and older) than I really was, I gained power as a leader. I did not lose any credibility at all. You can't fake being who you really are. When people see that you have the guts to show who you really are, they respect you even more as their leader.

You need to be aware of your company's culture. Wearing shorts at IBM would be as wrong as wearing a pinstripe suit every day at a start-up. But within the constraints of your company's culture, people respect leaders who are actually real people, who enjoy their life on the weekends, and who are not just portraying the image of a perfectly turned out, businesslike, extra-professional executive robot.

I really encourage you to have one brand that spans your work and weekends. The brand can be the same; the behaviors can be tuned for work and nonwork environments.

For more help on developing your personal brand, see "Standing Out" in the Resources on page 268.

The Hard (and Important) Part

If you like the idea of developing and using a personal brand, be prepared: defining it can be a difficult task. If it feels really hard to do, you are doing it right! It can take a lot of time and work to get a really solid definition of your personal brand. But once you do it, it will help you go faster, be more decisive, and be more effective in all your interactions.

It will remind you to put your best foot forward all the time. And it will give you the confidence to do so!

Having that checklist of how to behave in both ordinary and challenging situations will seriously help you build credibility and visibility as you grow your reputation and career.

Next . . . Sure, what matters is your competence,
but what about the people who only see you?

12. Look Better!

"Was He the One with the Bad Haircut?"

OK, it matters what you look like. I'm not talking about a beauty contest or a fashion show. I'm talking about the value of making it look like you invested some thought and effort in your appearance. And I'm talking about making sure that there is nothing about your appearance that distracts people from recognizing your competence.

A big part of your personal brand is driven by your appearance. Your appearance can immediately convey two specific things about you that have an enormous impact:

1. **"I Care."** Do you look like you made an effort? If your appearance gives the impression that you made an effort, you put points on the board. Before you even open your mouth, you have presented yourself as someone who invests effort in things. If, on the other hand, your appearance is haphazard—sloppy grooming, ill-fitting clothes, or generally just thrown together—the first thing you are saying to someone is "I don't really care."

2. **"I Get It."** Are you up to date? If you walk in with an up-to-date hairstyle, eyeglass frames, and clothes, you come across as engaged, relevant, and connected. If your style is a holdover from twenty years ago, what impression do you think that gives? Before you even open your mouth, you are saying, "I don't get it."

Why would I want to hire someone to represent a piece of my business who doesn't care and doesn't get it? You have a big hole to climb out of that you could entirely avoid by putting the right thought and effort into your appearance.

Whether you are interviewing, selling, or leading, why not instead stack the deck in your favor by investing in your appearance?

Do You Actually Care?

Perhaps you are reading this, thinking "I have never been one to care about fashion or style. As long as I meet the social standards of decency and address temperature and environmental hazards by covering the appropriate body parts, I have done enough. I see no point in spending time, money, or energy on fashion."

That is fine if you are getting all the opportunities, consideration, and success you want. But if you are getting blocked or striving for more, this is an important tool in your toolkit. Don't underestimate it.

Look Like You Made an Effort

A major factor that distinguishes people who look like they make an effort from those who don't is whether or not their clothes fit them well and were purchased in this millennium. Clothes that are too big look sloppy and make you look larger than you are, and clothes that are too small, too short, or otherwise fit wrong make you look incompetent. Clothes that are basically the right size but have no structure to them make you look disorganized.

You can make a big difference in tuning your appearance to your advantage, even if your work outfit is jeans and a polo shirt. If your jeans are a current style and cut, and fit you well, and your polo shirt is new and the right size for you, your look gives a positive impression. If your jeans are too short, too tight, too big, or old-styled, or your shirt is baggy, stretched out, or faded, you look less competent.

Is This Agony for You?

If you enjoy paying attention to fashion and style, and you know how to get clothes that fit your particular shape, than this is easy and maybe even fun for you. But if you don't know how to do this, it can be one of the most elusive and baffling tasks you have ever faced. Perhaps you have already tried, without success, so you've lost confidence in the process and fallen back into whatever habit of dressing you have been in forever.

The most straightforward solution is to go to a department store and have a personal shopper dress you. This is a free service at most department stores (though of course you pay for the clothes you end up choosing). Call ahead. Tell them about yourself and let them help you. Don't worry—they won't turn you into a ridiculous fashion spectacle. They specialize in bringing out the best in you. This has an enormous impact on your self-image as well as the image you present to the world.

It doesn't matter what your age, size, shape, or weight is. Clothes that fit *you* will make you look good. Never go for the baggy option. You may think you are covering up the "bad parts," but in reality, you are making your whole self look like someone who is hiding, someone without confidence—generally a negative impression. If you have trouble with fit, you will be amazed how much you can improve your appearance if you get some professional help from a personal shopper and a tailor.

It's not about having to look like a supermodel and wearing the latest trends. It is about wearing clothes that fit, which make you feel great, so you can present yourself as a competent, relevant person, no matter what your starting point is. And at a minimum, it is about making sure that no part of your appearance distracts from your competence.

Accessories

Details matter. A good watch, a good piece of understated jewelry, or a good pair of well-cared-for shoes—these go a long way to convey that you appreciate quality; conversely, cheap knockoffs of all these things convey that you are a hack. An unusual heirloom or a quirky but classy element can also convey that you are thoughtful and interesting—and again, that you have put purposeful effort into your appearance.

Make Sure Your Appearance Is Up to Date

Another critical factor in showing that you care and you get it is to make sure you come across as current: no Alexis Carrington suits or acid-washed jeans.

Clothes

If you harbor a sense of pride that you can still fit into the same trousers you wore in high school, good for you—just don't actually wear them! Spend more than $100 on a pair of new jeans, even if you think that is ridiculous or offensive. You will be surprised at how well they fit and how good you look. And you can afford it if you haven't bought a pair of new jeans in fifteen years.

Get new eyeglass frames too, at least every four years. Your eyeglasses are right in the middle of your face! Why would you skimp here? Pick something that brings out the best in you and reflects your personal brand.

Hair

You know who you are. . . .

Women, if you have had the same hair style for twenty years, it's time to give it up, especially if it involves curling your bangs under with a curling iron and then poofing up the hair on the top of your head and cementing it there with hair spray. Go to the salon. Get a current style.

Men, gray hair is fine as long as your haircut reflects the current style. Go to a real hair salon. Pay $50 or more. Or just wear it super short. Good news—bald is acceptable and current at any age. And if you don't want gray hair, please, please, please go to the hair salon. If you think it's embarrassing to go to the salon for hair color, at least make sure to take a big mirror outside in full daylight and check out your home dye-job, and then decide which is more embarrassing.

Facial Hair

Men over forty-five, if you grew facial hair in your twenties to look older, let me break the news to you—it is still working.

Makeup

Women, make sure your makeup is up to date. Get your makeup done professionally every two to four years. Styles change, and you change. If you've never done this, it's free at any department store. If you never wear makeup, give it a try and see what you think.

Age Doesn't Matter as Much If You Are Current

I have hired people in their fifties, sixties, and seventies who appeared to be more current than people in their forties. Anything you have had for twenty years needs to go!

Fragrance

In the last chapter we talked about standing out and being memorable. You want to be memorable because you were the one who went to Sri Lanka and built a school. You don't want to be memorable as "the one with the bad aftershave."

My experience with this is that no matter how wonderful you think your perfume or aftershave is, someone will be allergic to it or irritated by it. Every single time that this has been an issue, the person has been laughed at and remembered as "the one with the bad perfume."

If you use any kind of fragrance, use it sparingly and get some unbiased feedback from someone in an elevator with you before you wear it into an interview, sales call, or meeting. Or to be safe, just skip it.

Your Appearance and Your Personal Brand

If your personal brand is about being cutting edge, you'd better not be wearing sensible shoes, khaki pants, and a sweater vest. But if your personal brand is about being straightforward, frugal, or no-nonsense, there is no reason on earth that you can't have basic, classic clothes that fit you really well.

Your appearance speaks for you. You may think that your brains and your interactions are more important than your appearance, and they are. But what about the people who only see you? The ones you don't get to talk to—they count too.

When you go through the exercise of building your personal brand and managing what you want to be known for, your appearance is a factor in conveying that. Manage your appearance on purpose. Determine whether you need to make some changes in your appearance to better present your brand.

* * *

The Hard (and Important) Part

The important thing here is to not get stuck in a rut. People who are not into fashion can tend to get comfortable with how they have dressed for decades; they don't pay any attention to how that is translating today or ever bother to get any feedback.

Make sure that your appearance is serving your goals. Ensure that there is nothing distracting from your competence. If you are selling yourself, or aspiring for more, put some focused effort into your appearance. Go to the professionals!

Next . . . How to manage the key influencers
who can support or blacklist you

13. Be Visible, But Not Annoying

If You Get Ignored, You Get Blocked

I have seen people do almost everything right in their career, yet still get overlooked, blacklisted—or buried in a reorganization. Their once-promising career stalls, or worse yet, goes backward.

I can think of one guy in particular who worked in a large commercial software company. He was used to being a star performer. He was well respected and liked by his boss and his peers. But then his company did an acquisition. Everything around him changed. His boss left. The management structure grew as new people came in. He got pushed down two levels from where he was before. No one consulted him on the changes or considered him for the new top roles.

Don't let this happen to you.

To stay on a forward course in your career, and to be effective in general, you need to have visibility and support beyond your team and your direct boss. You need people above and around you to see you as someone who matters. When the world gets complicated, you need them to advocate for you or to come to your defense; otherwise you can get burned.

There Are Two Key Groups Who Matter to You

Your stakeholders are the people directly affected by what you do: your boss, your clients, your employees, your partners.

Your influencers are a bit less clear. These are the people you are not directly connected with but who still have a say in what happens to you. Your boss's peers and your boss's boss are good examples.

You have two choices:

1. Leave their perceptions of you to chance.

2. Proactively communicate with them and manage what they know you for.

KEY INSIGHT: *Leaving the perceptions of stakeholders and influencers to chance is one of the mistakes that can completely block your career from advancing—really. Focus on this before you feel like you need to.*

Visibility and Communication

So far, in the LOOK Better part of the model, we've talked about credibility, relevance, and personal brand. You can think of these as the "back office" work for your LOOK Better strategy. This is the part you do first—the introspective work to decide what you stand for. You create your plan to build credibility and to become more relevant. You develop your personal brand so that you can use it as a guide to be more consistent in your positive behaviors.

Visibility is the "front office" work. It is about getting your brand out into the world so that the right people know who you are and develop a favorable view of you. Now is the time to take your show on the road and make sure you are not invisible.

Decision Makers Don't Know You

If you operate in your own department most of the time and don't have personal relationships or functional reasons to talk to your boss's boss, your boss's peers, and leaders of other organizations, you can consider yourself invisible. And you can consider yourself stuck.

Many people feel that they need to leave their company to get a promotion for one simple reason: at the new company, the interview process is set up to give you an opportunity to sell yourself to the decision makers.

KEY INSIGHT: *The trick is to create that opportunity in your own company. Create opportunities to sell yourself to the decision makers in your company. This doesn't always happen naturally. No one may line this up for you. It is up to you to create that opportunity.*

How Promotions Happen

You need to be thought of as better than your peers.

Many people can't understand why they don't get promoted. It remains a mystery why some people get promoted and others are passed over.

Think about it this way. Imagine you are sitting in the staff meeting your boss goes to—her boss's meeting where your boss attends with her peers. There is a discussion of a new job opening up at that level. This would be a promotion for someone at your level. Your boss will be getting a new peer.

If the people in that room don't know you, it's tough for your boss to sell you to them—particularly if the people in that room already see your peers as highly competent and trusted.

KEY INSIGHT: *If you want that job, you need your boss and your boss's peers to think you are the best candidate.*

In fact, your boss's peers need to view you as more capable than their own employees! The stark reality: I have been at that executive meeting, where I knew all the people who were being considered. Frequently, the most capable person was immediately disqualified simply because no one knew him. The conversation quickly centered on the people who were known.

> **KEY INSIGHT:** *When the executives talk about who is the best, the people whose names are known (even if nothing else is known about them) come out way ahead of the more-talented people whose names are not known.*

Results First—The "Not Annoying" Part

You've probably noticed that I've mentioned this a few times, but it bears repeating. It's about results first, not visibility without results. (This is how you make sure you are not annoying.)

This also helps you get past any of the concern or hesitation with the self-promoting feeling of creating visibility. Make sure that first you are delivering excellent, remarkable results.

I am suggesting that you deliver excellent results but then *don't forget to let the world know what you have done.* The full impact of your good work on the business and on your career progress will be lost if you remain invisible.

Building Visibility

Many people struggle with this idea of building visibility. We are taught from a young age not to brag.

But in business, no matter how you feel about it, invisible doesn't work. So you need to come to terms with the fact that you must do something to create positive visibility. If your intentions are honorable and your results are strong, you are not doing a bad thing by creating visibility.

In fact, you are building genuine value by getting yourself and your team on the radar screen. It's not just about pay raises and promotions. People with high positive visibility have high credibility, and they get all the benefits we've discussed—better projects, more resources, more support for who they get to hire, and better cooperation from other teams. So they get better business results.

Even if you have no aspirations whatsoever to get a promotion, you are doing your work and your team a disservice if you remain invisible. You can be doing a fantastic job, but if some of your key stakeholders either don't know about it or have an incorrect, not-that-impressed perception of your work, it can be a huge block to your success and your ability to get promotions and resources for your team members or approval for projects you care about.

Creating visibility for your top performers is important too. By doing so, you are giving credit where credit is due, and you become known as a leader who can recruit, motivate, and develop stars.

Create a Stakeholder Communication Plan

I suggest creating an actual communication plan to ensure that you communicate with your stakeholders and influencers. You can use this simple worksheet to get started.

Stakeholders and Influencers	What Is Relevant to Them?	Your Desired Outcome	Form and Frequency

1. Identify Your Stakeholders and Influencers

Stakeholders are people who have a direct interest in or dependence on the work your team puts out. Your boss, your employees, and your partners all fall into this category. Influencers are the people who don't depend on you or have a structural reason to follow what you do but can have an impact (good or bad) on what happens to you. Often, your boss's peers fall into this group as do leaders in other organizations.

You need to have a clear view of who all of your stakeholders and influencers are. This is worth some special focus if you have not already gone through this exercise.

The usual suspects are your boss, your boss's peers, your boss's boss, your boss's boss's peers, external partners, customers, finance, operations, sales, and employees.

It's different in every environment. Really consider your environment, then make your list. Think about who your current work touches. Think about the job you want. Think about who that job touches. Think about people who would be good mentors, which we'll talk about more in chapter 15, Get Help. Note actual people's names. If you don't know names, note the roles and find out the names.

2. Create Your Strategy to Be Relevant with Each Audience

For each stakeholder and influencer, think specifically about what their goals and desired outcomes are. When they come to work in the morning, what do they care about most urgently? What keeps them up at night? How does what you do translate to meeting their desired outcomes?

Remember, talking in their language about things they already know and care about is what is relevant to them. Any planned communication will backfire on you unless it meets the following criteria:

1. Relevant

2. Competent and trustworthy

3. Not boring

Also think about the scope of what they worry about. If it is your boss, your issue may represent $1/8$ or maybe even $1/3$ of what they worry about. But if it's your boss's boss, it may only be $1/30$. If it's the CEO, it might be $1/2000$. Keep this in mind when you request time or build communications. Be sure to fit your communications into their context and be sensitive to the scope of what they worry about. If you try to get too much time for something that is just $1/500$ of what your audience cares about, you will lose credibility before you even get started. For example, don't ask a CEO for an hour. You will lose all credibility just in making that request.

The 7-Minute Meeting

As an example, I have found that with high-level executives you can build credibility just by requesting a short meeting. I request seven minutes and get it done in five. You will get noticed for your precision, and if you get it done on time, you may be invited to stay longer. Either way, the executive will love you for being brief and to the point.

I recently heard a great story from a midlevel executive in a consumer packaged goods company who tried this "7-Minute Meeting" idea with great success. He was tasked with one of those unenviable jobs that required getting executive input and signoff from about twenty very senior vice presidents—the kind of thing that could take the rest of your life. So he tried calling each one's assistant to request seven minutes with their executive.

Each one said, "Seven minutes—yeah, we can squeeze you in for seven minutes." Within a few weeks he had met with all of them. He told me that if he used his typical approach of asking for thirty minutes or an hour, he would still be waiting to get those meetings!

Never Talk to an Executive When He Has to Go to the Bathroom!

I once saw a female manager track down a male executive and demand that he talk to her. He said, "I'm sorry, but I am on my way to the men's room." She did not relent. She followed him to the door and tried to get him to not go in. When he made his final apology and left her standing in the hall, she ran around telling people how rude *he* was.

Look at your list and start to build your communication plan, but keep in the back of your mind that although this is really useful for you, you need to also make it useful (and not annoying) for *them*.

3. Identify Your Desired Outcome with Each Stakeholder or Influencer

Think about the outcome of getting visibility with this person. What do you want to happen? What do you want them to know or think about you and your team and your work? The intersection of what is relevant to them and your desired outcome will define the strategy and the content of your communication with them.

4. Determine How and When to Communicate with Each Audience

Once you have the list of your key targets and your communication strategy, think about the venue and timing. What is the ideal form and frequency of the communication that will be most effective?

For your boss, it may be a regular one-on-one meeting and a quarterly report.

For your CFO, it may be a plan to drop in every two weeks and have a five-minute conversation plus deliver a spending and outcome report every month.

For you partners in other business units, it may be lunch quarterly and a brief email update each month.

Think about what you want to accomplish and what their needs, interests, and communication styles are, and then structure a communication plan to get in front of your key audiences on a regular basis.

In my case, after not getting my pay raise because "nobody knew me" (as described back in the Introduction), I created a goal of having people know me and recognize the great work my team was doing. My communication plan had three major components:

1. Get personal introductions to stakeholders across the company.

2. Get personal introductions to influencers across the company.

3. Publish a brief written report each month that gets my name and the accomplishments of my team in front of a wide audience on a regular basis.

I delivered this report monthly to about thirty executives across the company for about nine months. I tried to make it engaging, but I'll be honest, it was kind of boring and not relevant enough. I could do it better if I had it to do over again. But even though it was not a brilliant work, it had a nice color graphic on the front and my name in large color print. (This was in the days of hard copy and interoffice mail.)

When I went to a company-wide meeting for the top leaders in the company, all of my "targets" were there. I took the opportunity to walk up and introduce myself to as many of them as I could find. I often got the following reaction: "Oh, hi, you're the one that sends that report on software with the color picture on it. . . . I don't read it, but I recognize your name."

In reality, this is 80 percent of what is necessary to go from being invisible to being known! And the briefness and regularity of it scored me some points for being credible and trustworthy.

A Good Plan Has a Variety of Contact Methods and Styles

If you are executing a communication plan well, you won't just send a report to everyone or call everyone on the phone. You will tune both the content and the medium of the communication for each key audience or person. It will result in a combination of reports, phone calls, lunches, drop-ins, formal meetings, and introductions.

It is important to meet people where they are, with information that is relevant, in the manner in which they like to communicate.

Be Brief

Do make sure to be brief. You do *not* want to be known as the person who has nothing better to do than to write long reports! I will tell you that in every large organization I ever managed there was always at least one person who wrote a five-page report every week about what was going on in their world. Don't be this person!

Communicate on Purpose

Put your communication plan into action by making sure it has owners and dates. When live discussions or meetings are required, make sure you get them scheduled. Have your team help you create the reports and deliverables, and engage them in the process of reaching out to your stakeholders.

I recommend starting out by spending two hours a month on this. Once you get rolling, you will find that it gets easier. The time you spend planning your communications will not exceed about two hours a month, and the time you spend actually communicating will become part of the natural course of your doing business. You need to be communicating with these people to get stuff done anyway.

Even though it takes some time on the front end, planning ahead ends up saving you loads of time and trouble by avoiding many reactive and defensive communications. And you save huge amounts of time when you need to get support from others. You are not starting from scratch, because you have made sure, through your communication plan, that they already know you and have an appreciation for the importance of what you do for them.

This is one of the things you must do as a leader to be working at the right level and supporting your team. You've got to step up out of the activity that consumes you and think more strategically about the position of your team in the company.

This builds your credibility and relevance and gives you a regular mechanism to reinforce your personal brand. It helps you execute better because as you build your visibility, you are building more and more support.

Being proactive about your stakeholder communication plan sets you up for greater success, both in doing your current job and getting the next one, and provides vital insurance against getting blacklisted or run over the next time the organization changes.

KEY INSIGHT: *Don't be invisible because you are too busy doing good work to share it!*

Mandatory Fun

I get a lot of questions about team-building exercises, happy hours, department lunches, and so on. How do these fit in with being visible? Managers wonder, "Should I schedule a bunch of these, or are they a waste of time?" Employees wonder, "Do I need to go to these? Are these as important to my career as getting my work done?"

As a manager, I think you need to do some of this. Social team building is helpful to create an effective working team. It also gives people visibility they might not otherwise get, with each other and with management (and you can and should invite management).

I have one strong suggestion for managers: *if you do this, do it during work hours*. Don't make people give up their free time, especially on a weekend, to come to a social work event. It's not *that* fun.

I recall one group of employees. The same people always came to these team-building events; there were other people who never did. The ones who never showed up complained that the other group got more time with management. They noted that we always did happy hours and that they had child care obligations so they couldn't participate after work. So we moved the gathering to 3:30 p.m. Guess what? All of the regulars still came, and all of the complainers were still no-shows!

Force yourself to show up once in a while. You are always better off not being invisible.

What If You Work Remotely?

Many people today are in a position where they don't get to see their boss or others in the management structure because they are working in a remote location.

If you are remote, it is up to you to not disappear.

Make Your Presence Felt

You need to go the extra mile to be seen, heard, and recognized. Here are the things that I would do if I had to exert my presence remotely:

- If travel is possible, spend a two- to four-week period with the main part of the group up front. Remote work becomes far more effective if people know you first than if they've never met you.

- Be the first one to call in on conference calls. Greet each person who joins the call. Let everyone know you are on the phone.

- Don't join late and then stealthily do email while you half-listen to the meeting. Don't put your phone on mute. Be fully engaged.

- Look for opportunities to drive the conversation or lead projects. Put yourself at the center of initiatives and issues so people need to reach out to you.

- Use video conferencing as much as possible.

- Send pictures every now and then.

- Have a list of people you reach out to every week without fail (part of your stakeholder communication plan).

If you are remote, it doesn't mean you need to be invisible. You just need to be extra rigorous with your stakeholder communications.

How to Communicate with People Above and Around Your Boss

Many people ask me, "What if your boss prevents you from contacting her boss or her peers?"

If you have a boss who is very controlling and unsupportive of your making connections above or around her, this goes back to one of my base premises: you can't blame your failure on the fact that your boss is stupid.

You need to communicate with influencers who are above and around your boss. There are two good ways to do this that do not get squashed by corporate hierarchy or cause conflict with your boss.

Positive Feedback and Thank-Yous

A really great way to meet people is to give them positive feedback and thank them for something. But you need to pay attention so that you have something on which to base the feedback. When you identify people you want to meet, look for places where they communicate—articles, all-hands meetings, public presentations—and study their work. Get to know what is important to them and what business initiatives they are driving.

Then give them some real, positive feedback. It's really important that this not be hollow and generic. You can't just say, "I saw your talk and thought it was really good." You need to prove that you were really listening, by saying

something like, "I saw your talk on how you studied supply chain optimization in the company that shipped bananas, and the learning you applied to your
technology business. That was really relevant for me because I was trying to solve
an inventory timing issue in our business. Thank you so much for sharing that."

As an executive, you don't get a lot of *thank you for doing something great*
emails—a few a year, maybe. This is a fantastic way to get your name in front
of an influencer in a really positive way. They will most likely write you back
and thank you for your message. You have then made a connection. If your boss
finds out and says, "I told you that I forbid any contact whatsoever," you can
respond by saying "because it was just a thank-you, not related to the business,
I didn't realize you needed to approve it." But at that point you've already made
your connection!

Then you can find opportunities to keep the connection fresh by asking for
advice specific to something you noticed that they recently did or accomplished,
by offering some information of interest, or by giving more feedback from time
to time. Remember, be visible but not annoying. If you can't personalize your
communication to something of specific relevance to them, skip it for now and
do more research.

Nonbusiness Points of Interest

In addition to giving positive feedback, if you can find a completely nonbusi-
ness hook to offer your influencer something of value, you can go even further
to build your visibility.

I have one example that had a big and lasting impact on my career. I saw an
executive two levels up from me give an all-hands presentation. I knew I wanted
to meet him, so I really listened to what he was saying so I could find a hook.

The next day I sent him an email and gave him positive feedback that I was
really impressed with his no-nonsense approach to managing expectations and
execution; I also mentioned that I had shared his struggle for not being able to
find good New York pizza in California but had finally found one really good
place I could recommend.

I immediately got a reply thanking me for the message, and I got another
email from him the next day! He had gone to the pizza place that night and
loved it. Those two messages gave me enough of a hook to ask for a thirty-minute

meeting to learn from him more about how he set measures and consequences, which I was genuinely interested in.

Once I closed the deal on that meeting, I went to my boss and told him the story. I "apologized" saying "I wasn't trying to go around you, but it's just that none of this was related to business. First it was about the pizza and then we got into a conversation about his personal best practice of managing execution, which I'd love to learn more about." After a minor grumble, the coast was clear, and in my thirty-minute meeting I was able to close a deal with this executive to be my mentor, a relationship that lasted for years. We are still in contact. And we both still go to that pizza place!

* * *

The Hard (and Important) Part

The really hard part here is making the time to do this. This is an area I struggled with early in my career because the tasks involved to communicate with stakeholders never seemed as urgent or important as the tasks to deliver the work I was on the hook for.

But I can't overemphasize the danger of *not* doing this. What happens to most people (including me) is that they get burned. They get passed over, demoted, or blacklisted because of a misunderstanding or because they were invisible.

Then we have the conversation about the fact that they failed to build a network of support above and around them in the company. No one was watching out for them or advocating for them.

After you suffer a loss or a big setback, it becomes more personal—and much more obvious—that you need to make the effort to communicate with stakeholders. So you finally move it to the front burner. Try to prioritize this *before* you get screwed. It's worth it.

Next . . . You can't just *have* brilliant ideas;
you need to *sell* them.

14. Selling Your Ideas

Having Brilliant Ideas Doesn't Mean People Will Listen to You

Much of this book is about what you need to do to put yourself in a position to sell your ideas. But once you are there, you need to sell your ideas!

KEY INSIGHT: *You need to be able to communicate ideas in a way that leaves the people in the room both intrigued by your idea and impressed with you personally. Never forget that it's both.*

Selling Your Ideas

Whether you are presenting your business plans, selling yourself in an interview, or just trying to work most effectively, it is critical to communicate clearly and engage your audience in a way that motivates them. It's one thing to have brilliant ideas; it's something very different to be in a position to sell them.

To put yourself in a position to even get an opportunity to sell your ideas, you must deliver excellent outcomes on the most important things, as we talked about in DO Better, and you need to build credibility and relevance. This is the hard, foundational work you need to do in order to earn the right to sell your ideas to the decision makers and influencers inside and outside your company.

Once you have done this, and you have the stage, make sure that you really sell your ideas. Do the right things on purpose to stand out and to inspire confidence. You need to motivate people to listen to you.

Don't just stand up in front of a room. Decide how you want to be perceived. Plan how you communicate on purpose to be engaging. It's not just about being showy or a naturally great speaker. It's about being clear and being yourself. If you are thoughtful and reserved, you can still have a compelling presence and be really clear and motivating about what you are talking about if you do it on purpose.

Presenting or Performing?

I'm paraphrasing something that Simon Cowell (the one who was the real music industry pro on *American Idol*) said to an early contestant: "You do not seem to be taking advantage of using this stage to perform for millions of people. You are acting more like this is a tryout than a performance."

I got to thinking about how people go about communicating, presenting, and behaving at work, and I think this is such an important point: Are you performing when it counts? Or are you just presenting, clarifying, and getting through the information? Are you defensive—like this is a tryout or a test you need to pass? Or are you really owning it and using the opportunity to its full advantage?

It's a valuable insight: think of any communication as an opportunity to perform. And I don't mean a showy, disingenuous performance or one lacking in either data or quality. I mean a performance that is compelling because you really care about it and you invest in *how* you present, not just *what* you present, because it matters to you personally to have an impact.

Make Something Happen

KEY INSIGHT: *Own the outcome of the communication, not just the communication.*

To turn a communication into a performance, you need to think about not only what you want to communicate in terms of the content but how you will capture and hold their attention. Here's a good way to think about this: what would you do differently if you were taking responsibility for the outcome and the actions this communication drives, not just the transmission of the information?

- How will you motivate, interest, or excite them?

- How will they be entertained—or bored?

- What is the difference that you want this communication to make?

- How will people's point of view be altered if you succeed?

- What will they do differently?

- What will they remember about the topic—and about you?

This is one of those things that really sets high achievers apart. They have the ability to inspire others with their ideas—to cause motion and action with their words. They invest in the performance.

Get People Excited

There is a key difference between performing and presenting. It's important to learn the difference because each will drive a very different outcome with your audience. Here are some examples.

Performing a Product Roadmap Presentation

If you are *presenting* a product roadmap recommendation, your goal is to share the information clearly. You can show time lines, technology choices, product feature additions, costs, competitive data, and so on.

But if you are *performing* a product roadmap presentation, your goal is to get people excited enough about the future that they give you the funding now and continued support along the way. You might include videos of user experiences and requests, physical prototypes, an interactive demo, or mock headlines that trounce the competition.

Performing a Business Review

For these, we always spend so much time *presenting* the data—covering every detail and defending against every hard question in the financials. You are so much better off if you spend some time *performing* proactively, off the defense:

- How are you going to inspire your reviewers most about the business?

- What kinds of ideas will they personally respond to, over and above the numbers?

- Why do you personally believe in this business?

- What are the most exciting customer stories about how your products and services changed their business?

- What is your top salesperson doing that you are excited about replicating?

I'm not suggesting that you skip the data and put on a song-and-dance show instead of managing the business. But you can get a lot further with your stakeholders if you take responsibility and excite them with the right images and stories instead of only boring them with a straightforward presentation of data, progress, and plans.

Performing a Budget-Approval Presentation

If there was ever a reason to step up your performance, it's to get your budget approved. Loads of data and metrics will not help as much as exciting stakeholders about what they will get for the money and showing them how much you are personally motivated to make a big impact on the business. Even the most number-conscious executives will respond to a compelling story about something that transforms the customer experience or the market.

Invest the energy to get your creative, marketing, and salespeople to help you with content. One good story can be worth a thousand spreadsheet cells.

You Are Being Judged Harshly

Another important point to consider is that you need to understand just how harsh the environment you are in can be. You need visibility with upper management but you need to also recognize that once you are visible, you are being judged really harshly.

For example, if you get a chance to present to an executive a few levels up, suddenly you have visibility. Thinking about this as a performance is critical to getting a positive judgment. How will you manage it?

You'll want to make a good impression. You'll probably spend a bunch of time on the content. You'll make sure you have your story together—that there are no holes. You plan your strategy for what you are asking for, and you make sure it's supported by the data. You stay up all night working on your slides.

But as much as you plan and craft your content, it is only a fraction of what your executive stakeholder is paying attention to.

It's Like *The Gong Show*

When you are standing there in the front of the room with your newfound visibility, know that half of each stakeholder's brain is paying attention to your content, and the other half is going into a fairly harsh judgment of *you*. And that judgment is this: is this person any good?

If you do not capture your audience in a strongly positive way, part of their brain will be tolerating your content but the other part may well be thinking, "We should ultimately move this person out to free up a headcount for someone better."

If your content is good *and* you make a strong personal impression, they will be thinking, "YES! This is important work, and this is someone to watch— someone we should ultimately promote."

This is why it is so important to think of these opportunities as a performance. If your presentation is fine, clear, but not compelling, part of each stakeholder's brain will be thinking, "OK, this seems fine," but you will remain lost in a sea of workers, unremarkable and easy to ignore.

It really is that clear cut. It's kind of like *The Gong Show*—remember, the act comes on, and after a few seconds of performing they either get to proceed because they are doing OK or they get "gonged" off the stage.

When you get visibility, the judgment is either *out*, *ignore*, or *promote*. Even if you are not after a promotion, your need to strive for that judgment in your executive interactions, because the other two choices will not help you succeed in or preserve your current job.

How to Plan Your Performance to Be Engaging

Your goal is to have an impact, create value, and solve problems. Your job is not just to inform and convey the detail you have studied; it is to engage and intrigue and inspire confidence, support, and action.

The opportunity to present an idea is a gift, not a chore. Learn to set a very high bar for how you will perform so you take advantage of each opportunity to create progress. Don't be tempted into thinking that your idea is so good that any logical person, upon learning about it, would agree with you.

You need to put as much thought into *how* you will deliver your presentation as you do about what is *in* your presentation. The quality of the content counts, but the following things count too—*a lot*:

- Are you being clear, succinct, and compelling?

- Have you tuned the presentation to be highly relevant to each audience?

- Do you get to the point? Are you sure you are not boring?

- Have you made sure you won't be tempted to go on and on about details?

- Do you show strong personal presence?

- Do you show confidence rather than defensiveness?

- Can you deal with disagreements and attacks and not get drawn off track?

- Can you field questions succinctly and not get nervous?

- Can you continue to be succinct and not babble on and on when you get drawn off topic?

- Can you regain control of the conversation?

What If You Are Not a Natural Communicator?

If you're naturally good at these things, you are a step ahead of the game. If you are *not* naturally good at these things, you need a plan. You can't just *not* communicate. But as we talked about in chapter 4, you need to always put yourself in a position of strength.

So if you are just not a gifted communicator, but you must communicate, how do you keep yourself in a position of strength when you need to do something you are not so good at? One option that can work really well is to partner with a spokesperson.

I saw a very humble, soft-spoken inventor blow away a group of venture capitalists by using this approach of partnering with a natural communicator. This allowed him to stay in a position of strength as the brilliant person making the serious and meaningful contributions, but also to make sure his story came across. His story had four parts:

1. Here is this brilliant thing I have conceived, created, invented, planned.

2. I would like to introduce Mary, who will tell you how critical and relevant it is.

3. I will describe clearly what it is.

4. Mary will talk about the time line, impact, next steps, and required commitments.

It doesn't matter how you sell your idea as long as it gets sold and you are viewed favorably. As long as you trust your partner, you both win. You are both in a position of strength. Your partner gets points for communication. You get points for being brilliant. The project is shown in its best light. Neither of you takes anything away from the other. You build each other up more than either of you could do alone because you are sharing strengths. The idea wins, the project wins, you win. I have seen this type of partnership work many times in corporate situations as well.

Step Up Your Delivery

Here is a checklist of tips that stack the deck in your favor:

1. Plan and practice your opening line. Think about your audience and what they care most about. Know what words they use to describe what they care about. Use their words, not yours. Make sure that you have an opening line that connects with what they specifically care about, and rehearse it.

2. Don't bury the lead in your presentation. What is most interesting, exciting, or important? The brilliant archaeology of how you got there doesn't matter—put it in your backup material.

3. If you have slides, rehearse an opening line and a closing line for each slide—actually write them and build a practice version of your presentation, with the slides that precede and follow each slide with your key point on them. Step through the presentation, making only the key, take-away points.

4. Be prepared for naysayers, questions, and getting thrown off track. Practice responses to the worst, most challenging questions you can think of. Have a prepared approach to deal with people who are taking shots at you.

5. Give your audience very clear choices and make it really easy for them to do what you need them to do.

6. Be memorable. Find a funny story or a personal relatable connection with your audience. This can be at the beginning, middle, or end as it suits your desired outcome and content.

7. The big finish. Make sure you ask for something specific when you close. Point people in the direction of action and seal the deal. Get a commitment for the next step. Always end with action.

Don't Bury the Lead

Don't get too hung up on your content and your agenda. If you walk into a room full of people who are asleep after lunch in a boring all-day meeting, your "lead" is to wake them up! If you are in a room full of skeptics, your lead is to create a bridge. If you are in a room full of strangers, your lead is to build their confidence in you. Once you have done that, your next statement should be the most compelling point in your argument.

As noted in the earlier checklist, always be clear about "the lead" and make sure you don't bury it underneath too much content, detail, and irrelevant or boring discussion. Hit people between the eyes with what will change their world for the better, using their vocabulary—your "outside voice."

Fight the Bull

One huge pitfall people fall into is talking "smart"—using big words and long, circuitous sentences. It always amazes me how some people insist that sounding smart will impress people who will think they are more businesslike, experienced, or wise. There is sometimes even a kind of arrogance—"Well, I understand this perfectly, so they should too."

You can find these people easily. You have been in meetings with them (long ones). You have gotten emails from them (long ones). These people use words with lots of syllables. They use long sentences. They provide way too much background, and they create lots of abstractions.

They confuse sounding smart with being smart. They confuse sounding smart with taking action. They confuse sounding smart with adding value. And after talking to them, you are left wondering what happened or what is expected to happen next.

Never Confuse Being Clear
with Not Being Smart

A big part of your personal brand and your credibility is based on how you communicate.

> **KEY INSIGHT:** *Clarity drives action. Sounding smart only drives more talking.*

Invest in tuning your communications to be as straightforward as possible. You have a much better chance of selling your ideas and making a good impression if people can understand you! Don't bury the lead underneath complicated, smart-sounding, superfluous words (like "superfluous").

Don't say "utilize" when "use" will do. Don't say "consequently" when "so" will do. I cannot think of a single instance in a business conversation when using the word "bifurcate" is necessary, or better than saying "split" or "divide." Don't use the work "dialog" as a verb. You don't sound smart. You just sound verbose and annoying.

> **KEY INSIGHT:** *Being clear is not the same as dumbing down or oversimplifying. It is about making sure that the most important information is presented in a compelling, straightforward way. This is harder to do than using lots of big words. But it's how you make the biggest impact.*

There is a free online resource you can use to spot the bull in your writing. You can find it at www.fightthebull.com.

Talking versus Doing

Be on the lookout for people who want to talk without ever getting to the *so, here's what we DO* part. Call them on it. "That's interesting; what do you recommend we do?" When they reply, "I'm just making sure everyone knows this important information" say, "We are discussing achieving specific outcomes and planned actions; do you have a recommendation?" Don't tolerate smart talk instead of action.

Present actionable information. For example, don't talk about needing data on something. Ask questions like, "What decisions will you be making based on this data?" or "What action do you need this data to inform?" Then do the analysis, present the actionable answer, and offer the data as backup.

The more you are known for clearly communicating, focusing on action, and actually taking action, the more credibility you will build. You will build trust. You will build a stronger base of support for your ideas. You will be able to sell your ideas because they will stand out as ones that actually make things happen.

* * *

The Hard (and Important) Part

It actually takes some real discipline to get in the habit of selling, performing, and motivating instead of just talking or presenting. It takes a lot more thought and planning on the front end, and it takes guts.

You need to be willing to put yourself out there and engage people with enthusiasm. It might feel strange. It probably feels safer to just keep it low key and communicate the facts. But just know that you are doing your career a disservice if you don't step up. If you want to own and drive meaningful business outcomes, not just talk about them, you need to actively sell your ideas.

Next . . . Successful people are successful because they get a lot of help—not because they are too good to need it! Get access to the best opportunities, fuel your imagination, and get your network working for you.

Part 3

CONNECT
Better

Get Support

Successful people get a lot of help.
Develop your network without being political.
Get access to and win the best opportunities.

15. Get Help

Success Is Scary, Not Comfortable

If you are growing your business or career, you will be in over your head from time to time.

If you are advancing, at times you will feel like you are not qualified, you are not doing a good enough job, and you won't be sure what to do about it. If you feel like this, you are doing it right!

When you feel like this, you have a choice. Act big and pretend everything is OK (and risk failure), or get help, learn, grow, and succeed. The most successful people are successful, in part, because they get the most help.

Getting help will give you an advantage. It will widen your margin of success over those who fail to seek it out or either don't recognize it or refuse it when it's offered. The more help you get, the more successful you will be.

I have never been refused help when I've asked for it. It has never gotten me into trouble or damaged my credibility. It has only improved my ability to deliver. Asking for help actually builds credibility because you are proving that you know something because people see you learn it—and because you deliver! Your management does *not* want to be surprised by your failure after a long period of "It's OK, everything is going fine." As a manager of executives,

I am always suspicious when someone never asks for help, an idea, or an opinion. I do not think they are extra smart; I actually assume they are less capable and will not advance because they are unwilling to learn from others. Asking thoughtful questions and showing that you are learning creates transparency and builds trust.

From Failing to Expert in One Step!

My favorite story about this happened when I was first a general manager. I had a hole in my product line that my team recommended we fill by acquiring a product from another company. Although I agreed, I personally had no idea how to execute such a transaction.

My first thought was "I am in over my head. General managers are supposed to know how do this. All of my peers are making deals. I am going to get found out. I don't deserve to be a general manager. *I don't know how to do the job. . . .*"

My second thought was . . . get help! So I went to the corporate development team. I reviewed the business need and strategy with them. They gave me the deal approach, content, and documents I needed to negotiate with the CEO of the other company. (They never questioned my fitness as a GM; in fact, they were really impressed that I engaged them.)

In my first discussion with the CEO, he had all kinds of questions and demands that I didn't understand at all. Because I had "my help," I was able to say to the CEO, "You know, we have pretty strict policies in corporate development. The best way to get through this is for me to just note all of your issues and go back to them and get you an answer on all of these things at once."

I did that. Corporate development helped rewrite the terms, and I closed the deal.

The punch line: About a year later, I got a reputation for being one of the best deal makers in the company. My peers who "knew how to do the job" were not getting help from the experts, and they were making bad deals for the company on their own. Because I had a team of experts helping me, we made a really good deal, and I became known for being a great deal maker. Lesson learned: Don't suffer alone. Get help!

Two Crucial Types of Help

In this chapter we will talk about two crucial kinds of help:

1. Getting mentors to help guide you

2. Building your extra team to help you get more work done

Mentors

Building your career without mentors is like climbing Everest without a guide and a Sherpa. Sure, you can attempt it, but why would you? I could not have achieved what I did in my career without the help of mentors.

KEY INSIGHT: *You just can't work fast enough, at a high enough level of value, in a visible enough way, or connect with the right influencers without mentors.*

Mentors help you DO Better, LOOK Better, and CONNECT Better. This is one of the most important topics in this book. Let's talk about the kind of mentors you need and why. Use this chapter as a checklist.

Mentors You Learn From

You can't have too many smart people in your life. Here are some important areas to have smart people challenge you to step up and learn things you might otherwise miss.

Ensure That You Deliver

You are *not* expected to know everything. But you *are* expected to deliver. Those are two very different things.

You are expected to be able to recruit the support you need when you don't know something. Then you can learn how to do the things you need to do along the way and still get them done. Part of the reason you won your job is because people expect you to be able to find and get the right kind of help. Never risk your deliverables because you don't personally know how to approach or do something. Never suffer alone. Get help.

Advanced Learning

Think about your fund of knowledge on a particular topic. It comes from what you already know, plus what you can research on your own in a given amount of time, plus ideas and information you can get from others. The more people you can go to for information, the bigger your fund of knowledge. So you can solve harder problems, learn best practices, and get inspiration for innovations.

Grow Your Capability

Asking for help benefits you not just for what you are working on now, but also by increasing the longer-term capability of you and your team, as we talked about in the DO Better part of the model. It's often hard to see ways to step up and change the game when you are so busy *in* the game. Mentors can challenge you and help you see how you should be making your job bigger, driving transformations, conceiving new opportunities, and developing your team.

Expose Your Blind Spots

It's easy to get so tied up in your current work that you can lose sight of the reality of changing attitudes, business conditions, or the market landscape. Mentors can help you see the things you are not seeing, navigate the land mines, work through unspoken rules, and keep you connected to reality, inside and outside the company, so you never get blindsided.

Mentors in the Job You Want

It's important to have at least one mentor who is doing the job you aspire to. There are four really valuable things you can gain from these mentors:

1. They can help you learn the job before you are in it. They can expose you to and teach you about the real requirements and help you practice thinking about them. They can help you win the interview and be more successful once you are in the job.

2. They might even give you access to special project work at their level so you can build some actual experience before you are in the job. See also chapter 18, The Experience Paradox.

3. They can get you access to jobs like theirs when they come up because, being in that role, they get asked who to consider. If they are your mentor, not only will they be sure to think of you, but they will know how to recommend you. They can also provide positive back-channel references, which are critical. In this regard, mentors are also one of the keys to getting on "the List" for the top jobs, which I will talk more about in chapter 20, Getting on "the List."

4. Part of getting the job is showing that you fit there socially. Having mentors who are already there gives you experience relating at that level. So you'll know how to act, and you'll have practiced doing it.

Mentors Who Are Influencers

Mentors provide a direct line to a level of people you might not otherwise be able to connect with.

Sure, you need to be building your personal network directly (which we'll talk about in the next chapter), but mentors can expand your personal and professional network exponentially—not only in sheer numbers but also in usefulness.

When you ask mentors for a connection, you'll be amazed at what they come up with, and how willing they are to connect you with people who can provide referrals, recommendations, introductions, leads, sales, partnerships— all the things that make business go. Don't underestimate the value of this. These kinds of connections drive real success.

It's also really important to have a mentoring relationship with someone like your boss's boss, or your boss's peers. As we talked about in chapter 13, Be Visible, But Not Annoying, you need to understand who has an impact on what happens to you and proactively communicate the right things to them. If you can establish a mentoring relationship with someone in this circle, this is big-time extra credit. You will have a much better chance of being recognized and rewarded for your work because you have a high-level influencer in your corner who knows you well and is motivated to help you.

Mentors for Air Cover

You are most vulnerable when you are not connected. What happens to you and your boss in a reorg, a downsizing, or an acquisition? How many people care what happens to you?

Because mentors by definition care about you and your success, they will advocate on your behalf. When discussions come up involving judgments of your worth to the company, whether it's about hiring, budgets, reorganizations, or opportunities, the difference between having someone in those discussions talk about you in a positive way and having no one mention you at all is huge. Make sure you get a mentor higher up in the organization who cares what happens to you!

Mentors for a Safe Harbor

Mentors provide an excellent source of safe help with your toughest business problems.

"I Have No Idea What I Am Doing"

With a mentor you can say, "Help! I'm stuck! I have no idea how to do this"—and when you're in that spot, it sure feels good to have someone to say this to. It's even more likely you'll need to say, "I'm really struggling with this; can you see what I'm missing?" or "Do you have any thoughts about getting around this issue?" Chances are your mentor can help, and you've got your problem solved!

You've just raced ahead of the person whose ego was too big to get help, and there is no cost to you. I have seen many people over the years destroy their careers by putting their ego first, suffering in "smart" silence, and thus failing to deliver. They never progress above the position they struggled in.

Your manager should be able to suggest likely mentors for you. When you have no idea how to do what you have been asked to do, ask your manager, "Do you know anyone who has done a similar project you could connect me with? I'd like to get some ideas and best practices." This works; try it!

Types of People to Look for as Mentors

When you are thinking about where to find these kinds of people, here are some ideas:

- Look for people who work at an order of magnitude bigger scope or geographic range. You can learn the thinking processes and techniques they use that help them do a bigger job, so you can apply those as your business grows. (Conversely, learning from a mentor at a much smaller company can also be really useful.)

- Look for people who are two or three career stages ahead of you—at a bigger company or in a more established business or product line. This will give you ideas for how you must grow and build capability to scale with the business.

- Also, find at least one mentor who is ten to fifteen years older and way ahead of you career-wise who can act as a career advocate for you and share wisdom and support throughout your career. This person can be inside or outside your company or even in a different industry—it's the general business experience and wisdom you're looking for.

- Connect with talented peers in other parts of the business. You'll gain not only ideas for general leadership techniques but also fresh insights about how people in other organizations and roles view what makes your team successful.

- Seek out people who do your job in different industries. I know a supply chain manager in a consumer electronics company who developed a relationship in order to learn from the supply chain manager for bananas at a produce company! They both shipped things worldwide that weighed about the same, but the banana guy had much more time pressure because his product would rot after two weeks.

- If you are over forty, you also need someone in their twenties who is a master at the Web and social networking. You need to keep up with how the world is communicating. Don't get left in the dark ages of email. Know how to share information and engage your customers. The young people I get this information from think *I* am mentoring *them*! If you are young and an online master, sharing your expertise can be a way to give some real value back to your older mentors.

How Many Mentors Should You Have?

The first thought here is: Don't be too selective. The more the merrier. You'll want to establish significant relationships with a key few but, in general, seek out lots of them for more informal relationships.

Here are some useful targets:

1. Engage at least ten smart people every year informally.

2. Recruit one formal mentor as a career advocate every one to three years.

3. Make sure you have at least three business advisors you can speak with regularly each year.

Think about your desired outcomes in your business and career. What are you trying to accomplish? Then build a targeted list of people (or roles) who know those things and set out to meet them.

How to Ask Someone to Be a Mentor

Don't get hung up on the term *mentor*. You don't need to negotiate a big agreement or formal process. It's valuable to just buy a coffee for someone you can learn from and reap the benefit of their knowledge.

However, once you make a connection, if the relationship sparks, close the deal! If you can formalize it to the extent that you both acknowledge that the mentor cares about your success over time, the benefits multiply.

To get started, make it a habit that whenever you meet someone you can learn from, you create a reason to spend time together. You can say, "I have noticed that you are really good at [something specific]. Has that always come naturally to you? Or do you have a specific approach that you use? Could I buy you a coffee and ask you some questions about this? It would be a great help for me to be able to learn from you."

If it goes well, ask for another meeting. If that also goes well, you can say, "It would be great if we could do this regularly, maybe once a month or quarter. Would it be OK if I contacted you to set that up?" Then, if it feels OK, "Having you as a mentor would be really valuable to me."

You Need to Kiss a Lot of Frogs

Some of the meetings will go great, and some of them will be uncomfortable and not turn into anything. That is OK. My success record in terms of meeting smart people, having a positive interaction, and then closing the deal with them to be a mentor is about one in five. (Specifically, in about ten out of fifty meetings, there was a spark and a continued relationship. Pretty much all fifty prospects I asked said yes to an initial meeting.) The personal connection doesn't always work out. So you need to keep trying. But when you get even *one* who cares about you and is willing to make time for you, it's a big deal.

How to Make Sure They Say Yes

People often ask me, "What motivates someone to be a mentor? How do I get them to agree?" Here are a few approaches that have worked really well, both for me and on me!

1. Ask in a Way That They Can't Refuse

I got a phone call once that went something like this: "Hi Patty, my name is Ron. I am new to HP and just out of college. I'm on the distribution list for your Friday updates, and I want to thank you for those and let you know that you have become the voice of this company for me. I then looked into your background, and I have to tell you I am just so amazed and inspired by you, and what you have accomplished in your business and in your own career, and I know if I could spend even ten minutes with you I would learn so much and would be so grateful. Do you think you could spare ten minutes to meet me?"

Let's hear it for shameless flattery! You can't say no to that. But the other great part of this story is that after I said yes, I picked up the phone to call someone who was several levels above me, who inspired me, and used the same line on her. It does work!

2. Don't Ask for a Lot of Time

Ron asked to meet me for ten minutes. I have had people do the flattery part to the point of embarrassment and then say they want to have dinner with me. I don't have time to have dinner with my *mother*. Ask for an amount of time someone can easily say yes to.

3. Offer Some Value

Be appreciative of their time, be funny or interesting, be proactive, be open to their advice. I am always amazed when people ask me, or even pay me, for coaching and then act like they know everything and have no problems. This is very annoying and a waste of time for both of us. Listen to what they care about and are interested in. Offer inputs and insights that they will appreciate. Follow up and say thank you. It can be just a short email or a handwritten note if that is more on-brand for you. Just don't let their invested time go by unacknowledged. Let them know that you did something they suggested and it made a difference. Mentors love this.

Make Sure You Set Up Mentoring Relationships for Your Employees

As a manager, one of the best things you can do for your top performers is to encourage and help them to get mentors. Everyone needs someone to talk to who is not their boss or their peer, and you will be getting more of your business problems solved faster by giving your employees access to learning that doesn't always have to come from you!

Be a Mentor

Most people don't recognize that they are a mentor-in-waiting. No matter what your role, you have an opportunity and an ability to mentor others. Even if you are an individual contributor in a company, passing on your knowledge and experience to others helps you, them, and the business.

Don't take for granted what you know. You know impressive stuff. It just doesn't seem impressive to you because you already know it!

I remember the first time I was called into a meeting about mentoring; I was excited because I thought I was getting a mentor. I was stunned when the person asked me to *be* a mentor.

Everyone can and should be a mentor. Seek out opportunities to help others. This is important to keep the balance of give and take in your network always leaning toward "give." You can always help someone. Be a mentor.

Build Your "Extra Team"

Here is the second big part of getting the help you need to succeed. Sometimes there is just too much work to do. You need to take advantage of the numbers. The more help you get, the more successful you will be. People who invest in building their extra team can get people who don't officially work for them to do actual work for them. So they have access to more resources and support for what they are trying to accomplish. Without extra people helping you, your progress will be slower and you'll have less capacity to deliver value for your business.

I See It with Successful Executives

They build informal teams of people who charge to their aid faster than most people could type an email explaining the situation. If a new opportunity comes up or an urgent crisis needs to be resolved, suddenly people from all over the company are working on it with no hesitation. If you think about it, you've probably seen people who are masters at getting others to do work for them. You can do this too.

I See It with Successful Salespeople

They can get teams of engineers, sales consultants, legal people, financing people, and partners in other companies all "on their team," investing time and energy and working to close a big deal.

I See It in the Most Effective Managers

Their own team is stretched thin, yet they seem to effortlessly recruit help from people on other teams, and the people and their managers are OK with it.

I See It in High-Performing Individuals

They don't work alone. They get help. If they have a presentation to prepare, they don't just go start typing. They get the web and graphics people started making slides for them. They get salespeople sending them customer examples. They get input from others who have more experience.

Recruit Your Extra People

To get extra people working for you requires that you have influence and impact that extends beyond just yourself and your own team. And this requires a personal investment in people over time.

When people think about building their network, they tend to think mostly about people above them or around them as the most "valuable" ones to get into their network. But people who manage to build an extra team think much more broadly. They reach out not just above and around them, but also *below* and around them. This is how they develop a team of people to work for them who don't actually work for them!

Reach Out to People at Lower Levels in the Organization

If someone above you reached out to you and made a personal connection, you'd at least be interested, maybe even flattered. You might view it as an opportunity to get some visibility. It would be a welcome and positive occurrence.

So why not do this for others? It's way easier to build a strong network below you than above you. Don't let your ego get in the way. It's more than worth doing. Think about connecting with ten or twenty or fifty people at a lower level.

Make a genuine, personal connection. Listen to them. Hear their best ideas. They see important stuff that you don't see because they are closer to the reality of the work and the customer. This is a huge opportunity for you to gain an advantage by being more connected with reality than your peers or your competition (because most people don't bother doing this). It's all upside for you. You need their ideas and insights. If you foster this, you will find many of your best ideas will come from this group.

If you do this well, when you need help with something, you will have an army of supporters who are motivated to help you. But to win them over, you need to give them something they value.

Ten Ideas for Building Your Extra Team

1. Make a conscious effort to meet people. Learn their names. Say hello. Show respect. (This goes further than you might think.)

2. Seek input from people. Listen. Say thank you, even if you don't use the ideas. If you do use them, let the sources know, and tell them how it worked out.

3. Create opportunities for people to connect with you. Eat lunch with them; spend time in their world. Ride in the car with a sales rep. Spend a few hours on the customer support line.

4. Be a mentor. Be available to give coaching and advice. Be generous.

5. Introduce people to each other.

6. Invite guests to your staff meeting so more people know your goals and your work. Invite a peer and suggest she bring a team member.

7. Offer to help your peers' teams when there is an opportunity to add value or help out.

8. Hold brainstorming sessions for your business and invite people from all over the organization to participate.

9. Share knowledge. Start an internal blog, share insights, and encourage ideas and feedback.

10. Give credit where it's due (if you don't, don't expect to get help from these people again).

This last point is worth emphasizing. People want their work to matter. So make sure everyone knows who did the work, including the person's boss. Make sure all of them get credit for contributing to the important business outcomes they helped you with.

It's also worth noting that some of these people will go on to be big, successful, highly influential, and powerful people later. I know I have in my network people who used to work for me who are now the CEO of, or in the number two position at a sizable company.

Having Strong Support Is Required for Advancing

Another unspoken reality is one of the biggest factors people look for when promoting people to high-level positions: how much support they have. The higher you go, the more you need the support of others. As you advance, success becomes less about what you yourself can do and more and more about what you can accomplish through others. As an executive, your value is largely associated with your network, and your effectiveness is tied to the power of your network.

KEY INSIGHT: *If you are not seen as someone who has a lot of support, you will not be viewed as capable of doing a leadership job.*

Imagine you are going for a promotion to an executive role running a large program that spans many organizations. One thing the hiring manager will do is poll people at all levels above and below you and across the broader organization. They want to find out whether people trust you, think you are competent, and would be willing to get on board with the changes you need to drive.

I have seen many people get turned down for executive roles because they couldn't show that they had a strong enough network of mentors and an extra team inside and outside the company they could tap into for connections and help. These are fundamental qualifications for a job at the executive level.

* * *

The Hard (and Important) Part

When I tell you that asking for help is an asset, not a liability, it may seem counterintuitive. But asking for help is a fundamental trait of the most successful people. If you are not comfortable with doing this, you'd better *get* comfortable, or you will dramatically limit your ability to excel and advance. Don't let your ego get the best of you. Never suffer or fail alone.

Next . . . How to build a strong network
even if you don't like networking

16. Authentic Networking, Not Politics

Build Genuine Connections That Create Value for Both Sides

I was really surprised by something that was happening in my speaking engagements and workshops. I always ask for a show of hands: "Raise your hand if you are good at networking." In every single case, the vast majority of hands stay down.

This was a big "aha!" for me. I went through most of my career thinking that I was the only person in business who was not good at networking—and that therefore I was at a huge disadvantage. So I'm happy to report the good news: if you are not good at networking, you are not alone!

The other good news is that you can actually do a good job at networking if you are not naturally good at it. If I can do this, anyone can. People are always surprised to hear that I am an introvert. In fact, I score quite high on the intro-vert scale. But because I am expressive, people expect me to be naturally drawn to meeting people and networking. Not so!

Over the years I have developed systems and crutches to help (or force) me to network. And as a result, I have built a very strong personal and professional network that I continue to invest in and that pays huge dividends. After you do it for a while, it becomes easier and easier and starts to happen more naturally.

That's the thing about networking. Everyone always wants ideas for how to get better at networking, but in reality, you just need to do it. Networking is not one of those things you can master by thinking about it. You just need put yourself out there, do it, and learn as you go. In this chapter, I will show you how you can build a strong network, even if you are uncomfortable or not naturally good at it.

It's OK If You Don't Like Meeting New People

One of the biggest obstacles people put in their own way is the discomfort with meeting new people. They get into a mode of thinking that the only way to do effective networking is to meet a bunch of strangers and make high-powered connections with lots of people of influence. They build it up in their mind as a really big deal that seems so improbable that they don't bother doing any-thing at all. But that's overlooking one of the key lessons about networking that makes all the difference:

Network with People You Already Know!

Keep in mind that networking has two distinct parts:

1. Keeping in touch with the people you already know.

2. Meeting new people

Most of the power from networking actually comes from keeping in touch with the people you already know. Think about it. Even if you never meet another new person for the rest of your life, you can build real value into the network you already have. Meeting a new person is only the first step. You still need to stay in touch with them if you want to create any value from that meeting.

In this chapter we'll talk about how to do both types of networking.

> **KEY INSIGHT:** *Don't let discomfort with new people keep you from building value into the network you already have. Consider meeting new people as a separate task, one that doesn't prevent you from doing a better job of networking with people you know.*

Networking Is about Giving

One basic truth about what I refer to as "authentic networking" is that networking is actually about giving, not taking. This point of view really helps take away any negative political edge or discomfort often associated with networking. Once you start to think about building your network by what you can give, and by adding genuine value for others, it becomes much more meaningful and feels much less political. *Remember, your network only has value if you put value into it.*

> **KEY INSIGHT:**
> *The Networking Paradox:*
> > *You need a network that can help you; however, networking is about giving, not taking.*
> *How is networking about giving?*
> > *You build your network by giving.*
> > *You use your network by taking.*
> *The Trick to Authentic Networking:*
> > *Give when you don't need anything.*
> > *Take less than you give—always.*

Networking Part 1: Keep in Touch with the People You Already Know

Keeping connections fresh is entirely about giving. You are giving someone attention, and you are not asking for anything. It is a pleasant contact for them. And it makes a huge difference. If someone hears from you, even once a year in an email when you don't need anything, then when you ultimately do need something, it is very comfortable for both parties. But if you haven't connected with them at all in five years and suddenly, out of nowhere, ask them for something, it becomes very uncomfortable for you and potentially annoying or easy to ignore for them. You may recognize this situation from having been on one or both sides of the exchange.

If you have kept the connection fresh and updated, not only will it be much more natural and comfortable when you need to reach out, but the other party will be much more inclined to actually help you!

Several people who used to work for me check in once or twice a year; they let me know what they are up to, ask how I am doing, send a photo of their family or vacation trip. When one of these people needs a reference, not only am I really glad to do it, but I also do a better job of it than I would for an "out of the blue" contact because I feel like I am not talking about a stranger.

In contrast, there are a few people in my network who contact me every two or three years *only* when they need a reference, but then never follow up and say thank you or let me know what happened. In one case I had heard through the grapevine that this guy got the job. I sent him a congratulations note, asked about his family, gave him some ideas about people I could introduce him to who might be helpful in his new role—you get the idea. Never heard back. It got to the point where this guy contacted me four times over about six years for a reference, and I never got a single contact other than that. I will forgive people for being busy sometimes, but no one is too busy not to check in or say thank you even once in six years! I still get requests from him; I have just stopped responding.

Ten Things You Can Give Your Network

When I talk about giving things to your network, what I mean is making a connection, offering value, doing a favor, and not asking for anything in return. Here is a list of specific things you can do.

1. **Hello:** Just say hello or give people a quick update when something interesting happens. Be the one to stay in touch. You are not asking for anything. You like to hear from people; so do they. People appreciate it when you are the one to make the effort to stay in touch.

2. **Remember things:** Listen. Then follow up later: "Did your son get his black belt?" "Did you buy those Acoustic Audio speakers?" "How is your daughter doing in New York?" It feels good when someone remembers your details. When someone tells me something about their work, their hobbies, or their family, I put a note in my contact database, so the next time I connect with them I can remember and ask.

3. **Offer to help:** "What is your challenge right now? How I can help you?" I know some really effective salespeople who start every single meeting this way, asking, "Before we get on with the agenda for our meeting, what is going on with you, and how can I help you?"

4. **Positive feedback:** Most of us live in a professional world with very little positive feedback. How often does someone go out of their way to tell you they admire or appreciate you? When you do this, it stands out, is appreciated, and is memorable. "I was really impressed with [that article, that talk, something gutsy you did in a meeting]—It really made a difference to me. Thank you." Unsolicited positive feedback is a gift.

5. **Say thank you:** I can't tell you how many people *don't* do this. There are people I only hear from when they need a reference, and then after I let them know I gave it, I never hear from them again. Saying thank you is a big deal in your network. Thank people a lot and often. For example, keep a list of all the people you contacted during a project or a job search, and send out a note at the end letting everyone know what happened and saying *thank you.*

6. **Follow up:** When you ask someone in your network for something (like a reference, advice, an introduction) and she follows through, let her know what happened. Did you get the job? Did the idea work? Most people don't do this either. I do all kinds of things people request of me and I rarely hear back about what happened. When I do, it is the exception, and I am thrilled. Once I got a call from an executive recruiter while I was driving; a referral I'd made had led to an actual placement, and she wanted to thank me. I almost drove off the road! That's very rare, indeed.

7. **Make an introduction:** Be astute about helpful introductions you can make. By doing so you give not just one, but two people a valuable gift without asking for anything in return. Make sure, however, that it's valuable for both parties; introduce only people you are certain will both benefit from the introduction. That is giving. If you are making an introduction because one of the people needs help and the other can give help, just be clear; in one case you are giving and in the other you are taking.

8. **A point of interest or enjoyment:** If you remember what is important to people and what they like, it gives you an opportunity to point them to great stuff that you run across like articles, movies, books, music, and events. Food also works! (Remember my exchange about the pizza place.) These can be pointers to business articles or resources that relate to their work, or something you think they will enjoy personally, like pointers to music, videos, recipes, photos, podcasts, and so on.

9. **Photos:** It's amazing how much of a difference photos can make. A colleague of mine at an agency tried to get a response from a prospect for over a year. Finally he decided to attach a photo from a trip to Italy to one of his emails and he got a response within minutes, thanking him for sharing the photo and opening the door for a conversation. Use photos of things you've seen and done, yourself, your family. You always look at them when people send them to you, don't you? It is a real personal touch. But make sure to either send a link or resize them. Don't email 8 MB photos!

10. **Video mail:** Video mail is an excellent way to make a contact as well. And it comes across as a much bigger deal than it actually is! The trick is to think of it and do it. It is a personal and standout way to say hello to someone, and people remember it. Just search the Internet for "free video email."

The Power of Weak Connections

We all have key relationships in which the whole point is to spend time with the person because we enjoy and value that. These are our *strong* connections. You tell these people about your life, and you want to hear about theirs. You do things together. You know each other very well. The fact that this takes time is a good thing.

Weak connections, on the other hand, are with people you know who at one time you had a real reason to connect with, but now you don't have a regular reason to contact each other. Your weak connections are still personal connections. They are not just a stack of business cards of people you don't really know at all. And keeping those connections fresh is very important.

Among the many reasons we tend to resist connecting with people, (1) we feel like we don't have time to do it in the first place, and (2) we feel like we don't have time for the relationship that would occur if we made contact.

There are two really important considerations here:

1. A connection typically *doesn't* turn into a time sink—others are busy too.

2. Weak connections are actually very valuable.

How much time does it take? You can establish or maintain a weak connection about once a year with a brief phone call or email. In techie terms we call this a "ping." A ping is a test of a network connection. You test that both sides are there, but without sending any real data.

Here is an example of a personal networking ping—"I thought of you the other day, and wanted to say hello. Things are going well for me and my family. Still at my same company, but I started a new job as a regional director, which I am enjoying. Hope you are well." Use your own style, of course, but the point is to realize that this ping doesn't demand a lot of "data."

KEY INSIGHT: *Weak connections are about keeping the connection fresh, not keeping all of the details of the relationship current. So they don't take a lot of time. (I am here; you are there. I thought about you enough to acknowledge our connection.)*

The Value of a Weak Connection

A large network of weak connections is more valuable than a small network of close connections. And it is not just a matter of the numbers.

KEY INSIGHT: *The people you are close to are not always very useful to help you because they tend to be in the same environments, know the same people, and think similarly to you. Whereas your weak connections have access to different stuff!*

If you are on a job search (a big reason people reach out to their network) or looking for new insights, your network of weak connections will have far more new ideas, broader reach, and bigger impact.*

Networking Part 2: Meeting New People

We've talked a lot about building value into your network by keeping in touch with people you already know. Now let's talk about meeting new people, because to grow your network you have to do this too. And this seems to be the biggest hurdle for most of us. But remember, meeting new people is only the initial, one-time event. After that, you still need to invest value in staying in touch with them, or the new connection won't be worth anything as time goes by.

---

*There is a phenomenon called the "strength of weak ties" based on work by the sociologist Mark Granovetter, who studied the impact of strong and weak ties, specifically in job searches. I have observed this phenomenon for years, but now I know there is actually scientific evidence that it is true!

Have a Real Reason to Meet People

People who feel like they aren't good at meeting new people typically are uncomfortable with the process because they don't know how to start a conversation with a stranger or generally don't like networking events.

The good news about authentic networking is that it's OK if you feel like that, because you don't need to do those things. Collecting a stack of business cards from people you meet once at a networking event is not adding any real value to your network. If you hate this, skip it. Instead, think about authentic networking as making real connections with people whom you would actually like to meet and stay in touch with because you share a real reason to be connected.

Set a goal to meet people based on things that genuinely interest or inspire you. Then you have a real reason to meet them, and you already have a topic for the discussion. You don't get that uncomfortable feeling of engaging a stranger in small talk. And you leave with a real connection that you can build on over time.

I have grown my network significantly over the years, in a very authentic and high-value way, by reaching out only to people who have done something that has genuinely interested, impressed, or inspired me, and telling them that they had done so as my way of contacting them.

Here's how this goes. You contact the person and say

I [read an article, saw a panel discussion, listened to a webcast] where you [did something, said something]. I was very interested in [a comment about something you were actually interested in]. The reason I was so impressed was [insert a real reason].

I thought I would connect with you and let you know you had [some sort of positive impact on me]. If there is ever anything I can do to be of service to you, please let me know.

You will find in most cases the person will respond graciously. They may ask you to actually do something, and this is a great outcome, because then you can give something that will reinforce the connection. And whatever you learn from their response, put it in your contact database and make a note in your calendar for some weeks or months out to contact them again.

Done: You have added a real, valuable, authentic connection to your network.

This authentic networking approach also works really well at networking events. Instead of just showing up, figure out ahead of time who is going to be there, do some research, and then set out to meet specific people for specific reasons that actually interest you.

You will be way more comfortable at the event because you will have a sense of purpose and some goals—find and meet these three specific people—and you will be armed with something to talk about once you meet them. Skip the cocktail receptions if you don't like them and just set out to meet a few people you would actually enjoy meeting.

Making Time to Network

So how do you make the time to network—and then force yourself to do it?

I have created a very simple but systematic way to stay in touch with people, and this system serves as my crutch to make sure that I keep up with my network. I am a big believer in "crutches" because they help you do things that you ordinarily put off, have difficulty with, or are uncomfortable about. Life would be too hard if you could only rely on focus, determination, and diligence for everything. Building some crutches is what got me to become decent at networking after years of doing it poorly and being uncomfortable with it.

Schedule Networking Time

I can't believe that there is anyone who is too busy to schedule thirty minutes per month for networking. Think about how many emails you could send in thirty minutes: Five? Ten? Twenty?

Even if you sent only five a month, in the course of a year you would have made contact with sixty people! That is *way* more than zero for an insignificant time commitment. Pick an amount of time that is palatable for you and actually put it on your schedule.

For help on making time to network and building your networking plan, see "Networking" in the Resources section on page 268.

Getting Your Network Working for You

Now here's the part about using your network to get things you need. Be clear about this: you build your network by giving; you use your network by taking. Just always make sure to give more than you take. It doesn't need to be a one-to-one ratio; the general rule of karma applies.

As long as you have built up a good balance of value in the network bank by giving, you will be able to *take* without offending anyone, and they will be motivated to help you. But there are ways to do the taking so you optimize what you get and don't either burn network capital or offend people in the process.

Here are three rules of thumb when using your network:

- Be personal

- Be specific

- No dead ends

Be Personal

It's important to maintain your contact database, but be careful not to damage it with impersonal mass mailings.

An excellent example of what *not* to do is something many people do with LinkedIn. LinkedIn has a feature that allows you to send an email message out to your entire network saying "Can you endorse me?" I can't tell you how many of these I get.

Remember the number one rule of networking: give more than you take.

Using this feature is a mega-take! In one moment you ask every single person you are connected with to do something for you without offering the slightest value (or even saying hello) in return. Doing this is burning network value.

If you want to reach out to your network for help, personalize it. Go through your contact database and sort them into groups based on how well you know them and what you would be likely to ask them for. Personalize your group emails. Send lots of personal emails.

You can send two hundred individual, personal emails. If you do twenty a day, it takes a couple of weeks. And it makes a huge positive difference.

Be Specific

The more specific you can be when you reach out to your network, the more likely it is that someone will be able to help you.

KEY INSIGHT: *Be clear about what it is you offer, not what it is you want.*

Example: "I offer a consumer products company the ability to restructure their product offerings to capture more market share. That's what I do well. I am looking for introductions to people in these specific companies, recruiters, and anyone you know who could benefit from getting a revenue growth assessment of their go-to-market plans."

That is so much more useful to the person you are asking for help than saying, "I am looking for a marketing job. Know of any?"

KEY INSIGHT: *The more specific you can be, the easier it is for people to help you. It seems counterintuitive, but the specifics are what help trigger people's thoughts of where the connections are.*

No Dead Ends

The other thing you need to master when using your network for ideas, leads, and referrals, is never to treat any networking meeting or conversation as a dead end. When you go into any networking meeting, aim for these desired outcomes:

1. Give something.

2. Understand whether this person can help you and inspire them to do so.

3. Get them to introduce you to someone else who might help you.

Don't Leave the Meeting Without Doing #3

If someone says, "Sorry, I don't know any one who might be a good fit," and that is all you get, you have accepted a dead end. If instead you ask, "Do you know someone else I could talk to that might know someone?" more often than not you will get a referral to one or more new connections. Over a few months you can build a sizable network on a specific topic, even if you only start with a handful of people, if you always go into your discussions with the goal of no dead ends.

A Note on Social Networks

Social networks are useful and valuable. Social networks like LinkedIn help you find people and keep your contact information working. Facebook and Twitter are a great way to "ping" your weak connections. You can build value into your network of both close and weak connections by being present and generous on social networks, but they shouldn't fully take the place of direct live interactions and personal, one-to-one connections with key people in your life and work. And just like other networking concepts, they don't do the work for you—you need to put value in if you want to get value out.

* * *

The Hard (and Important) Part

What most people struggle with is making the time to build value into their networks when they don't need anything. When everything is going great, the motivation to connect with people (if you are not a natural connector) just isn't there. You are busy and focused on other things.

It's important to fight this tendency, step away from the work, and schedule some time to stay connected with people. If you don't, you will be very uncomfortable and embarrassed when you ultimately need your network after you've failed to stay in touch. You put yourself in the awkward and much weaker position of having your first contact in years be an *ask*.

You don't need to be a "natural networker"; just schedule time and start doing this. It gets easier as you go, and it is vitally worth it.

Next . . . You can't do great things
if you never think of them.

17. Imagine That!

If You Want to Advance, You Need Other People to Fuel Your Imagination

Why do some managers reach the C-suite level and others get stuck at the director level, even though they are equally talented and have done pretty much everything right?

Why do some careers thrive and others stall?

There's a hard reality we all need to deal with in our careers: even if you do everything right, you can still get stuck. Why some get their breakthrough comes down do two things: *imagination* and *fearlessness*. The combination of these two things is what allows those who make it to get beyond what every human faces from time to time—lack of confidence.

As we discussed in previous chapters, you need mentors and a strong network of support. You also need to proactively connect with people who challenge your thinking and give you great ideas. You need to connect with people who help you imagine what is possible and who make it all less scary.

Confident or Fearless: Your Choice

People often want big jobs, but they are unwilling to pursue them until they feel confident, comfortable, and "ready."

> **KEY INSIGHT:** *If you are not confident you can do the big job, you have two choices:*
>
> 1. *Spend time learning, getting experience, and checking all the boxes so that you will feel confident.*
>
> 2. *Be fearless and do it now.*

The first choice could take forever and you still wouldn't feel confident, because there is always more to learn and always someone else who you think is better.

The second choice gets you there. Fearlessness is partly about having the imagination to see yourself in that role, deserving that role. It is also about being willing to go there before you feel ready and comfortable. Over and over again, I have seen less-talented, less-qualified people move beyond higher performers for the sole reason that they were willing to do so.

Leap, Then Learn

Here is the trick: fearlessness first.

> **KEY INSIGHT:** *You first need to get yourself there. Once you are there, learn really fast, do the job, and get more comfortable and confident as you go. Then leap again.*

You can have a good career without doing this, but if you aspire to big things or the top jobs, you can't get there without putting aside your confidence issues and just doing it anyway. If you are smart, you will catch up with your leap. I promise. I've done this with pretty much every job transition I've made.

Imagine This: You Are Allowed!

People get really wrapped up in the fact that they do not deserve to be working in a bigger job. They think the world is watching and waiting for them to check all the boxes and will then escort them to the bigger role. It just doesn't work that way.

This is where the imagination comes in. It is only a failure of imagination that keeps you thinking you don't deserve to move forward yet. The world is not waiting for you to check all the boxes; they are merely watching to see if you'll step up.

The ones who step up and go for things are the ones who get them. The ones who are fearless get there faster.

Look back to chapter 15, Get Help, to make sure you have mentors who can help challenge your imagination, help you learn what the new job will entail beforehand, and encourage you to take big leaps. Looking back on all my biggest, scariest transitions, in each case I had a mentor telling me I should go for it (putting it in my imagination) and telling me I could do it (encouraging my fearlessness). I would have stood still much longer without this inspiration and encouragement. I wasn't sure that I could do it. I didn't feel I was ready or deserving. But with mentors telling me to take the leap, and by trusting myself to learn when I got there, I did it.

One of my mentors once told me: "Everyone who is a CEO has been a CEO for the first time. At that time they had no experience as a CEO. Why are you any different? Trust yourself." (Thank you, mentor!)

You Need to Fuel Your Imagination

Even in your current job, you need to make sure that you are not missing opportunities for bigger wins. Without imagination, you will not redefine your job to be the bigger and better one that needs doing. You will fail to add enough value to the business. You will be left behind when the business scales up.

Think about your job and its future . . . its payoff . . . its value. . . . What is the end game? What if the thing that will create your biggest success in your job is something you haven't thought of yet? What if the best solution to the problem you are working on is something you are not likely to think of on your own?

You can't get above the work without imagining what is possible instead. How will you make sure you think of breaktheugh options? Whether it's how you solve problems or how you create new opportunities, you can't do it if you never think of it! If you spend too much time in your current way of thinking, with no triggers or stimulation to think about things in new ways, you will miss many opportunities.

Most of my biggest successes have started from other people's ideas, challenges, or inspiration. They did *not* start with things that were in my own imagination before someone else helped put them there.

One of my biggest jobs ever, I was not even planning on interviewing for. A mentor said to me, "Why aren't you going for that job?" My response was along the lines of "Who, me? I'm not ready for that job." Then when he told me which other people were interviewing, I thought, "Well if *they* can go for it, so can I." But I wouldn't have thought of it myself.

One of the biggest problems I've solved in my career was in rebuilding a sales channel for a business turnaround. I knew it needed to be done, but without a mentor or partner with lots of experience in the regions, I never would have had the ideas for how to structure it to make it work.

Where do you get your ideas? Who challenges your thinking in a positive way?

Using Your Mentors

Let's go back to mentors. Really, don't try a career without mentors! They can help you learn things you don't know and see things you don't see. They play a critical role in fueling your imagination.

Even if you don't have official mentors, it's critical to regularly engage with a wide array of smart people at various levels, companies, industries, and ages, to make sure you have a steady source of challenges to your thinking and fuel for your imagination.

Mentors will help you always challenge yourself to think about how you can do your job in a bigger and more effective way—or reinvent it entirely!

Then Get Ideas from Everywhere Else Too

We've talked about many things that set highly successful people apart; the one I want to talk about here is this: they are excited by other people's ideas. They immerse themselves in input.

They are not satisfied with the status quo. They are driven to make things better, have a bigger impact, build excitement, improve processes, create new things. Most people who are highly successful do have a lot of brilliant ideas personally, but they also get a lot of input from others.

Highly successful people are always ready to recognize and accept a good idea from anyone. It doesn't matter if it comes from a highly paid consultant, a board member, or the person who comes in to clean up the catering after lunch.

They are excited about the ideas of others and are generous with appreciation, credit, and praise. This generosity and acknowledgment makes people want to help them.

So they have a wider and much steadier source of good ideas than people who either don't think they can learn from others or refuse to acknowledge when they do.

I have worked with many people whose egos prevents them from ever saying, "Wow, that's a good idea! I never thought of that. Thank you." These are not the people whose careers are soaring.

Build Your Pipeline of Good Ideas

Here are some ideas for building a steady pipeline of input for your imagination:

- Establish a habit of talking to people before you get to the end of the process of what you are doing, or before you feel like you know all the answers. You are more likely to be open if you are not most of the way down the road already.

- Start conversations assuming you know *less* than the other person. Even if you are certain that you know more, take some time to listen anyway.

- Stop yourself from saying, "We tried that already" or "We already thought of that"—that shuts off the flow. Instead, ask "In that case, how would you deal with this complication?"

- Talk to people you don't ordinarily talk to. Ask them what they think about—you'll be surprised how many new ideas this will generate. Ford Motor Company got the idea for the assembly line from the livestock butchery industry.

- Seek out excellence in other businesses and industries. Learn from people in other roles in other companies. Great ideas are rarely obvious. They come from being out in the world and being observant, curious, and open.

- Specifically seek out people who think very differently from you—the ones who annoy you because they are always on a different page. Meet with them regularly to discuss your work, your plans, and your goals, and get their annoying feedback. It might trigger a new way of thinking or working that you would never have thought of.

It doesn't matter where a good idea comes from. Just be sure to put yourself in the stream and recognize them when they come along!

You Have Permission

The other failure in imagination that I often see is that people don't imagine they are allowed to change their job and the business around them to make the future happen.

This is another imagination trap that sets the directors apart from the C-levels. They have big ideas, but they assume that the change would be too big and not supported. They feel like they don't have the permission to pursue it, so they don't even try.

This is another reason why it is so important to build your credibility and relevance, and put yourself in a position to sell your ideas as we talked about in the LOOK Better part of the approach. And it's another place were you need to demonstrate some fearlessness. Drive real change. Add real value. Don't wait to be asked. Imagine it, and do it.

Do the Job That Needs to Be Done, Not the One That Is Given to You

In chapter 2, Ruthless Priorities, we talked about redefining the workload to add the most value to the business. In chapter 4, The Agony and the Paycheck, we talked about renegotiating your job description to put yourself in a position of strength. In chapter 6, The Level Dilemma, we talked about stepping up to give yourself a chance to work *on* the business to make improvements to strategy, systems, and processes. And in chapter 8, Better with Less, we talked about reinventing how you do the work to deliver more value with fewer resources. Do you see a theme here?

It's up to you to change your job.

As people step up to higher-level roles, there is an outright expectation that they will not just do the job as it stands today. They will understand where the business needs to go, and they will reinvent the job to get there.

You need to get your imagination telling you what needs to be done. You need to challenge yourself and to give yourself permission to drive change. Make the job what it needs to be to add the most value. Get above the work.

* * *

The Hard (and Important) Part

No one is going to guide you here or make room for you to do this. No one will be inviting or directing you to invent the future. As you advance, you need to realize that not only do you have permission to do these things, but it is expected, and higher up it becomes *required*. That *is* the job!

To stand out as a leader, you need to imagine what is possible, set the right course, and then drive significant changes to get there.

If you rely only on your own ideas, you will have a disadvantage in creativity and confidence. When someone triggers something in your imagination that you could never have conceived of on your own, and they help you realize you can actually do it, it changes the world for you. You must cultivate this kind of connection with others if you plan to advance.

Next . . . How to connect with others to
go after and land your next big job

18. The Experience Paradox

How Do You Land the Job When You Don't Have the Experience?

You know you are ready for the promotion. You know you can do the job. But you keep getting told you don't have enough experience.

Many people get frustrated, believing that getting promoted is a purely political exercise, and they become resentful at being passed over when other equally qualified (or less qualified) people "who know people" get the good opportunities.

Truth be told, sometimes it does work this way. If you can develop a relationship with someone who will take a chance on you when no one else will, that is one way to overcome this challenge. But there is also a practical way that you can take direct control for solving this problem yourself.

Get the Experience before Getting the Job

You have to proactively make new connections for yourself that enable you to get the experience you will need to advance.

KEY INSIGHT: *You can't get the job before you get the experience, but you can get the experience before you get the job.*

It's important to realize that you can't expect your current job to give you all the experience you will need for the job you want. So the big idea is that you need to get new, different experience in the job you want *before* you are in it, while you are doing your current job.

I have seen many people miss the boat here and encounter the following pitfalls, which can stall your career for years, if not forever.

Avoid Getting Too Much of the Wrong Experience

I coach a lot of people who want to be general managers. Here is an example of someone who was doing this wrong.

Marla was an operations manager who wanted to be a general manager. She told me that she had several years of experience in product development, and she was now an operations manager. After a few years she was planning to try to get a job in marketing. She asked me, "What other functions should I get experience in before I can go for a general manager job?"

Marla was making the mistake I call "collecting all the cards." The flaw in her plan was to get experience in pretty much everything except general management!

KEY INSIGHT: *You don't want to get experience deep in the content of what your desired job manages; you want to get experience in the job itself.*

You are wasting a lot of time. Your competition isn't doing this. You are not learning how to do the job you want—in this case, general manager. You are learning how to do marketing, or finance, or supply chain, or R&D.

> **KEY INSIGHT:** *What you need to know is how to* manage *these functions, not how to do them. You need to be able to set and lead the agenda for business growth. You need to make tradeoffs between those functions, not within them.*

Although it is not necessary to get experience in doing all of the jobs that your target job manages, having experience in more than one area is helpful to broaden your perspective. For nonsalespeople, sales is the most helpful function to add to their experience. Any executive is much stronger after having spent significant time with customers where the business really happens. Spending time in sales changes your perspective forever, for the better.

When I interview candidates for non–sales positions, sales experience always scores extra points, because people who have had responsibility for making the business happen directly with customers are transformed—they have a sense of reality that does not exist for people who have spent their whole career at headquarters.

> **KEY INSIGHT:** *Time spent in sales helps you make better business decisions and become a stronger business leader. Not every general manager has spent time in sales, so it's not a must, but the ones who have certainly have a leg up for both winning the job and doing the job once they are in it.*

Avoid Getting the Level Wrong

If you look back to chapter 6, The Level Dilemma, you'll see the importance of understanding that at each level the game changes. Not only are the skills different, but the values are different. What you care about, what you measure, and how you lead are all different at each level as you go up.

If you are running customer service for one product in one region, realize that the job of running customer service for all products globally is a totally different job. You are not optimizing process, cost, or customer care for your product anymore; you are making tradeoffs to achieve the right business model for how to invest in service across all the product lines. You will need to take resources away from some products and give them to others.

You will need to understand regional and cultural issues. You will need to negotiate budgets with a CEO who is making tradeoffs between services, product development, marketing, and sales. You will need to choose regional leaders who can optimize customer care and profitability. It's a very different job.

If that is your goal, you don't need to get more expert in running services for other individual product lines; you need to really learn what the bigger job is and get some experience taking on work at that level.

How to Get the Right Experience

Now we can move on to the things you can do and the connections you need to make to get the right experience. The basic idea: identify the experience you want and go get it. Where is it? Think about what we talked about in chapter 2, Ruthless Priorities—successful people don't do everything. So that means for whatever job you want, the person doing it is most likely not doing a complete job of it. That's your opportunity. You need to go get some of that work. Do it well, and voilà: the next time you interview for the job, you will have actual experience.

This is one of the reasons it is so important to make more time, as we talked about in chapter 3. If you are completely consumed by your current job, you will not have any time or energy to do the things you need to do to get a better or bigger one.

And remember, you can never sacrifice the quality of your results or slack off on doing your day job. You need to use the techniques in this book to get your current job done in less time so you can make room to do more. Nothing happens without that.

Here are four techniques for getting the right experience for the job you want.

1. Find People Who Are in the Job and Learn from Them

As you are working to build your network, set a goal of meeting as many people who do your target job as you can. Invest in them. Learn from them. Spend as much time with them as possible. Meet them where they are. Make it pleasant and fun for them to spend time with you. Offer to cook them dinner, and learn from them while you are cooking. If they are active, suggest going on a hike with them.

Spending time with people at their jobs is critical. Find out what it is really like to work at that level. Here are some questions to ask them:

- What do you think it takes to be good at this job?

- What do you think is the hardest part?

- What is the most challenging issue?

- What corporate issue, rule, or program is most annoying to you?

- What business drivers do you react to first?

- What business drivers do you affect directly?

- What is the biggest problem you have overcome?

- How do you set goals for your team?

- How do you find stars and identify low performers?

- What do you seek to learn about the competition?

- Where do you invest to add value or extra quality?

- Where do you cut cost to drive efficiency?

- How do you communicate with your organization?

- What are the most important peer relationships?

- What has worked well in leading a team of this size?

- What has not worked?

- What would you do differently if you had the chance?

- What best practice have you discovered that you can share?

- How does your organization deal with changes in course?

- How do you process direct feedback from customers?

- How do you interact with the sales force?

- What does the CFO bug you about?

- What are the things you would like to fix but can't get to?

- What elements of what you do drive revenue, cost, and profitability?

- What elements of what you do, do other organizations depend upon?

- What do you believe you should stop doing but are forced to continue?

- What do you believe you should start doing but can't get support for?

I could go on all day!

That's the point. Meet as many of these people as you can and learn as much as you can from their experience.

2. Use Other People's Experience

When I started doing this, it worked so well, I couldn't believe it! Once I was interviewing for a CEO job and was asked a question about "How would you handle X type of situation?" Because I have been meeting and learning from CEOs for years, I had lots of their experience to draw from. So I answered, "I was just talking to a CEO who had a similar situation a few weeks ago. It was fascinating, because at first he saw this as one issue, but then he realized there were two: first, a clear external issue to be solved, and second, overcoming significant internal resistance to doing this.

"It's my sense that the situation would be the same in your case because [...]. He did [the following three things] to solve the external issue as quickly as possible, knowing it would require further follow-up to make it stick. At the same time he invested significant energy in an internal communication program for everyone and a specific training program for the sales and support organization.

"He also made sure that marketing did a consistent external and internal launch. It worked pretty well, but [the one big gotcha was . . .]. But he was able to solve that after the fact by renegotiating with the key partners.

"If I were in that situation, I would do exactly the same thing, but I would bring in the partners up front."

It worked like a charm. Since then I have used this basic strategy over and over again. Use other people's experience as if it were your own. You are not lying, because you say up front that someone else did this, but it gives you a chance to prove that you know what to do and would go in with a plan.

But for this to work, you really had to be listening and you really had to learn what happened and why things worked out the way they did. You have to own the learning and build it into your worldview. You need to articulate how you would do something similar so you can talk about it with as much detail and confidence as if you had actually done it yourself.

3. Practice Your Next Job before You Are in It

I've found this technique very helpful throughout my career. I was always in sight of the job that I wanted, whether that was the VP of marketing early in my career or the general manager/CEO job later in my career. If you really pay attention to what that person in your target role does, what she is confronted with, what decisions she has to make, how she makes them, and how it turned out, you will not only learn a lot, but you can play a game with yourself to actually practice making decisions for that person.

I did this (literally) for years. When I was in the staff meeting with my peers, after I made my contribution, I did not check out. I carefully watched the interaction of the general manager with all of my peers—with the manufacturing guy, with the finance guy—and with his peers from other organizations.

I tried to get underneath his questions and the issues and really feel what it would be like to be in his shoes. What seemed easy? What seemed hard? How would I make that decision? Why did he ask this question? Why didn't he ask this other question? I would ask the other question and either help the whole team or learn why that was a stupid question. I made all the decisions that faced the GM before he did. I kept track of what happened when we agreed and when we didn't. Sometimes I was right; sometimes I was wrong.

But I was learning to think like a general manager. By the time I started interviewing for general management positions, I had been practicing thinking like a general manager for several years. I can't tell you how much that helped me in my interviews. I had loads of general manager thoughts and experiences to talk about.

4. Get Actual Experience in Your Next Job before You Are in It

This is really what you are aiming for. Because you can't expect your current job to give you all the experience you will need, you need to figure out what specific experience you require, find it, and go get it yourself (without sacrificing quality or results in your current job).

If you have done all the other steps, you should be in a position to have relationships with people in your target job and be able to see and suggest or ask them if there is any important work that they are not getting done that you can help with.

Make sure it aligns with your strengths, and make sure it will be experience that will help you specifically go for the job you want. Don't just take on extra work that needs to get done if it doesn't align with your goals. You are already committed to your day job. Your extra work that you volunteer for should serve your personal purpose to get ahead.

Here is how I did this. I was in a huge turnaround situation in a failing business that was losing a lot of money. So although my official job was running marketing, I put on my general manager hat. I looked at the business more broadly and determined what we needed. We needed a new strategy to do the turnaround. I also determined that we had lost the sales force. We needed to reengage and remotivate them. I found that the business had lost focus in the regional organizations, so we needed to hold business teams accountable in each region. We also needed a media spokesperson.

As the marketing leader for the business, I took on all of that, but I did it from the point of view of "How would a general manager assess these challenges and lead them?"—not just from, "How would a marketing person deal with these things?"

I set the Ruthless Priorities of establishing a new strategy, creating a sales channel in the regions, and building confidence in the marketplace with customers, media, and analysts. (Note that I let a lot of marketing stuff go undone; although it was really important, it was not as much of a Ruthless Priority. My bet paid off.)

On all of these, I cast my net more broadly than my official marketing role, because that was what the business needed, and I racked up significant general management experience, even though I didn't have the title. I found the opportunity to do these things because the general manager was fighting other fires. The general manager, my boss, had real strengths in product development and operations. He was also, rightly, not doing everything. He was focusing on *his* Ruthless Priorities to get the product program sorted out. So I was able to work out a deal with him that I would cover the strategy, sales, and communication areas. It was a win for both of us.

By the time I interviewed for the first general management job I won, I was ready. (I had tried but failed earlier, because I didn't have the right experience.) By this point I had loads of general management experience. I took it upon myself to get the experience before I got the job and then used that experience to get the job.

Don't Assume You'll Get All Your Work Experience at Work

I love this story. I talked to a woman who repeatedly got turned down for second-level management positions. She was told "You don't have any second-level management experience."

Because her current job, as a first-level manager, was not providing her with second-level management experience, she volunteered to become the president of a nonprofit organization with two levels of management below her.

After about six months of doing that, she was able to change her interview to include not only her great strengths, skills, and results but also her specific second-level management experience and accomplishments. She could talk about leading the new organization from a position of experience. She got the job.

Smart lady.

This Is What a Development Plan Should Be

We all work on development plans for ourselves and the people who work for us. What I have discussed in this chapter is what a development plan should be.

- Decide what job you want.

- Go learn about it.

- Find projects that give you experience in that job.

- Get support from your boss to take on those projects.

Just think how much more productive that is than an employee coming into your office and saying, "Can you help me with my development plan?"

What if instead they came in and said

- This is the job I ultimately want.

- I have been learning about it.

- I know this person who is in this job and I would like to offer to help him to do X as part of my development.

- Can I get your support?

Then you can actually help! And that employee's development plan is owned by the right person—the employee, who's actively taking responsibility for developing a successful career.

* * *

The Hard (and Important) Part

Most work environments don't make career development obvious or easy. Don't wait for help. You'll be better off if you consider yourself to be on your own. If you know what job you want, get busy meeting people who have a similar job. Learn about it, and negotiate projects that will give you the experience you need. Start getting recognized as a candidate by taking on the right extra work and getting some visibility. Don't wait for your manager or company to make this happen for you.

If you are not sure where you are heading but know you want a change from where you are today, invest time in meeting people who do different jobs so you can start to learn which ones are most interesting to you. Waiting for someone to point you in the right direction won't get you anywhere.

Next . . . How to compete for and
succeed at a much bigger job

19. Going Big

It's Different at the Top—Don't Miss It!

This chapter is about to how to go after and win a big job. You need to understand who has influence in filling the top job and to connect with them in a way that shows you are ready for the big leagues.

I have very specific experience with this. I have targeted and won multiple C-level jobs in my career. And I have been the decision maker in filling dozens of executive roles. I know what stands out, what works, what gets ignored, and what gets laughed at.

Hint: It's Not about the Work!

Each time you take a step up, the world changes—a lot.

When you interview for a big job, you need to show that you get it—that you really understand the view from above the work. I have interviewed many talented people who might have been able to do the bigger job, but you wouldn't know it from their interview or their lack of executive presence.

To win the executive interview, there are some things you must avoid doing at all costs and some things that you must do. We'll talk about both. But before that, I want to talk about the general concept of executive presence, because you won't get to the table without it.

Executive Presence

Executive presence comes naturally to some people, but probably fewer than you think.

People often say to me: "Well, this is easy for you; this is one of your strengths." I can tell you this was not always so. I can remember early in my career being very nervous, timid, or awkward in certain situations with top executives, and being worried and defensive when I had to meet or spend time with "important people."

Because I was always young for the job I was in, I was often coached that I needed to work on my "gravitas" or executive presence. So for much of my early career, my executive presence was not easy or automatic. I had to work on my executive presence. I eventually got there and it became very natural. I promise, it gets easier. You can get there too.

Executive presence has four elements:

1. How you feel

2. How you look

3. How you behave

4. Ease and grace

How You Feel

This goes back to what we discussed in chapter 4, The Agony and the Paycheck. First and foremost, be who you really are.

If you are being true to yourself, you will be comfortable. You will come across as strong. If you are trying to contrive a false executive persona, it will be much harder to pull off—and impossible to maintain even if you can pull it off. You need to be confident. The best way to be confident is if you are leading with your natural strengths. This makes you your most powerful, and it makes you most comfortable.

Comfort and Confidence

This is really the crux of the matter. It's hard to be comfortable if you are not confident. There are two schools of thought:

1. Go into therapy for years to work on your self-confidence.

2. Do it anyway—be fearless even when you are not confident.

Many years ago, I read an interview with the comedian, singer, and improvisational performer Wayne Brady, which had a big impact on me. To paraphrase, he said that when he needs to do anything on stage, if he is confident about it, he does it full on, all the way, and it turns out great. But if he is standing on stage thinking, "Hmm, I'm not sure this one is going to work, or I'm not sure this is going to be good"—he also does it full on, all the way, anyway.

His message: Don't ever back off, even when you are not confident. It never helps to second-guess yourself and approach a performance apologetically or tentatively in case it might not work out. Backing off never makes your performance better.

In fact, being cautious about what you are doing is guaranteed to make it worse. I have thought about this every time I was in a situation where I was not as comfortable or as confident as I would have liked to be about my role, my performance, my argument, or my task, and I can tell you, *acting confident anyway* makes a huge difference. Just going for it, full on, is always better than the moderated, apologetic version.

Executives Don't Know Everything

There is no executive who knows everything about the job she is in. Executives are successful because they are willing to put themselves out there, make presentations, make decisions, and lead even though they don't know everything personally.

The people who scramble around to learn and master every detail are the ones who get stuck, because

- It is an endless task....

- So it uses up all your time....

- And you never actually step up and get around to leading.

These people believe that they can be competent (and therefore confident and comfortable) only if they know all the details. But they are sacrificing their executive presence and failing to lead. Think of it this way: by definition, this goes against building any executive presence, because people always *see* you in the weeds.

How You Look

When you walk into a room, if you want to be seen as someone who is in charge, someone with presence, you need to look the part. I have seen executives who are very casual get away without this, but these were people whose confidence and other leadership behaviors are off the charts. If you want to stack the deck in your favor, pay attention to your appearance. We talked about this in chapter 12, LOOK Better! Have a plan.

No one ever felt more confident by wearing a cheap suit.

In fact, I heard that when Sean Connery first started playing James Bond, they got him a really good suit and then encouraged him to wear it all week and even sleep in it. This goes back to feeling comfortable. Sean Connery pulled off James Bond, in part, because he was comfortable in his suit!

How You Behave

How you talk and act, and what you say and do, either builds or degrades your executive presence. Being comfortable and confident gives you a huge head start, of course, but the specifics matter too.

Whether you are in a room with your team, at a large function at your company, or in a meeting with your executive committee, board, or other big, scary people, it is important to show up as a leader with strong presence and be recognized as such.

Step up!

If you are in a room with your team, lead. Step up. Don't just be in the room or at the dinner with them. Say something. Have a point of view. Reach out to them. Bring them together as a team with your words and actions.

If you are in a room with big executives, step up. Meet them. Get a sense of what they are most interested in and talk to them about that. Ask some questions. Get input and feedback. (Fearless, remember.)

If you stay in the shadows or are timid because you are nervous about being there, you are only showing them you don't really belong there. Be willing to engage.

Ease and Grace

No matter how you may feel, you should never *appear* overwhelmed. In reality, this is part of how you behave, but it's worth highlighting separately. A key test of executive presence is to look like you are doing your job with ease and grace. Even if behind the scenes it is chaos, what people should see is you being calm and in control. If you appear overwhelmed in what you are currently doing, you are by definition showing that you are not ready for a bigger job.

- Deal with what is overwhelming *privately*.

- Don't cancel meetings at the last minute; don't act rushed and impatient.

- Don't get upset or defensive when people do things that throw you off course. Just say, "Let me take that input and get back to you." Then go off privately and scream, get frustrated, rework or not. Go back calm and in control.

Things You Must Avoid When Interviewing for an Executive Position

In addition to working on your confidence, fearlessness, and executive presence, here are some specifics that you must avoid in interviews for big opportunities.

Avoid Talking Too Much about Your Experience

What you have done in the past is not what is going to make you successful in a new and bigger job. If you talk about it too much, you come across as not understanding the job you are interviewing for.

The things that made you successful in the past are, by definition, things that are at the "wrong level" for the new job. Sure, you can demonstrate some wins and success, but if you spend too much time talking about what you've done, as collateral for what you will do in the new job, you will lose.

You need to show that you understand what it takes to work at the right level in the new job. This is why it is so vitally important to have mentors who can coach you, to meet and learn from people who have been in that job, and to get some experience at that level before you are in the job interview (as we talked about in previous chapters).

Avoid Talking about How You Solve Problems

If you talk about how you solve problems at a lower level in the organization, that won't get you very far in your executive interview. Instead you need to be talking about how you will lead the people who solve those kinds of problems. Demonstrating that you will work at the right level in the new job is critical.

For example, if you talk about how you fixed problems in the channel and increased margins, that is great story for a director. But if you want to be viewed as a VP or C-level candidate, you'd better have a game-changing story. Your story needs to be more like how you will strategically reevaluate the overall channel because you feel like you have the wrong mix of partners and that is causing you to miss significant market opportunities.

Avoid Presenting Yourself as a Package of Skills

A more junior, unseasoned person will walk you through the things on his resume, and talk about his experience and skills. Presenting yourself as list of skills and experiences is boring and unimpressive.

Instead you need to go back to your core strengths, as we talked about in chapters 4 and 11, and get to the essence of what makes you good at what you are good at. If you are good at supply chain management, is it because you are driven by not wasting anything, because you are highly analytical, because you get to the crux of problems, or because you sort out complexity?

KEY INSIGHT: *Everyone interviewing for the job will have the job skills. What makes you special? What values drive you to do what you do really well? What is at the essence of what you have done well over and over again in every job that you have had?*

That's the interesting stuff! That is what you need to talk about in an interview. When people hire an executive, they want to know the person and what drives that person to work and achieve.

Who you are as a person, what motivates you, and why you are good at what you do become progressively more important as you move up. Your experience and skills become progressively less important because the big jobs are about leading and motivating people and creating an environment where your team can thrive—not doing the work personally. If you talk too much about your skills, you will wash out.

Avoid Long Discussions about Tactics

Get to the punch line, please.

Put an executive filter on everything you say. Don't say you are *highly technical*. Don't tell the story about how you worked through the weekend creating a piece of code that had an impact on the business, no matter how much fun you thought that was or how proud you were of that.

Say *your technology background improves your business judgment* and helps you see opportunities. In the case of the weekend coding, *you recognized a market need and got a solution in place. The business won.* You find that your technology background also helps you *go faster, compete better against the competition, and get more out of the engineering organization.*

Don't say you are *great at marketing.* Say "Yes, of course I'll handle all the marketing stuff, *but the strategic issue for the company that marketing needs to address is the aging of our brand, our corporate story, and the impact of the Web and social media on our position in the market relative to new players.*"

If you want to be an executive, you need to talk like an executive in your interview and resist talking in detail about the tactics that won you your many prized accomplishments, because those stories are at the wrong level.

Avoid Not Fitting in Socially

If you want your seat at the table, you can't stick out like a junior, awkward guest in the room with your potential peers. You need to fit in socially and be able to interact comfortably at their social level. This is a specific aspect of executive presence.

This is definitely a consideration for who gets chosen. They will want someone they feel comfortable with, who can stand up with them as a peer, intellectually and socially. (Clearly, having a mentor already in that room will give you a huge advantage.)

When you get interviewed for a junior role, you will be asked about your resume. When you interview for a senior executive role, you will often get questions like, "So, how's it going?" The interviewer will then sit back in the chair, fold her arms, and be quiet. This is a social test. You better not start babbling at this point, going on for a half an hour about your skills and your background. You need a snappy answer that is something like, "Things are going well in my business. We just beat our largest competitor in North America, which was a key goal for us. I am also, right now, very proud of my daughter who just got accepted to Juilliard. And I've just started working out with a new trainer at the gym—he's about killed me, but I'm actually enjoying it. I am eager to discuss this opportunity because I have done some research and have some ideas about growing the business that I want to share, no matter what the outcome of the search is."

Cool, thoughtful, in control: you are a well-rounded human, highly competent, ready for a bigger job, and with a life outside the office.

You will get vague questions like "Tell me about yourself" or "What's your background?" Be prepared, be snappy, be impressive, and at all costs, don't be boring!

Avoid Being Boring!

I have interviewed hundreds of people seeking executive and senior management positions. Virtually all of the people were qualified—more than half of them were boring.

In addition to *not* presenting yourself as a package of skills (boring) and *not* going on endlessly about tactical detail (boring), you need to craft what you say about yourself so that you leave a strong, positive, unique impression. Your goal is to be engaging and intriguing and to leave people with a "sticky" story that they will remember. Here are some examples:

- Boring: I have a lot of experience leading complex projects and programs. I always deliver on time.
- Sticky: I am very competitive, always have been. So I make sure the goal is not only clearly defined, but looming large, to motivate the team to cross that finish line, because I am so driven to win. A great example of this is a funny story about when I was racing Italian motorcycles....

- Boring: I have led service organizations for technology companies for fifteen years. I have experience in software and hardware.
- Sticky: I have an unusual combination of strengths. I am both highly analytical *and* hugely action oriented. I can analyze a lot of information quickly, but then I'm driven to *act*—not to get more data. This has always been true about me. An interesting example: In college, I created and ran a children's marine science competition....

- Boring: I have exceeded quota for twenty-seven quarters in a row.
- Sticky: I'm kind of obsessive about maximizing success in any situation, and I have an unusually strong sense of empathy. Customers love me because it's always clear that I am creating and fighting for exactly what they need. As a result, I've never missed a quarter. There was this one time when a customer really wanted to buy from me, but I could sense she had a conflict that had nothing to do with the business. I was amazed at what I learned....

Don't skip the weird stuff!

I know a sales manager who had a former career directing theater. I know an engineering manager who is also an award-winning chef! Everyone who interviews them knows it too.

It's as important to be memorable as it is to make a good impression in the first place. "Is that the one who does competitive origami?" gets you far more traction than "Is that the one who said they are good at delivering products on time?"

Things You Must *Do* When Interviewing for an Executive Position

In addition to avoiding the hazards just listed, there are some critical things you must *do*.

Do Prepare the Right Stories

Don't just walk into conversations and wing it. There are critical stories that you must prepare to support your executive-level discussions. They are stories that

1. Convey *why* you are good at what you do

2. Describe game-changing initiatives

3. Get the scope right

Story: **Why You Are Good**

The higher the position, the less the work skills matter, and the more it matters who you are as a human, what your values are, what your natural strengths are, how you lead, and how you choose and develop people. Sure, you need to cover the skills to get the interview, but to win the job, you need to convey *why* you are good at what you do.

By discussing your core strengths and values, you show people what they are going to get when they get *you*. You give people a sense of depth that they can trust. You are sharing not just what you have done, but *why* you are good at what you are good at. Also, let them know *why* you always deliver in a certain way because your core values and strengths drive you to do that over and over again. It gives them a sense of what they can really expect from you.

This is how to win over a partner. This is how to introduce yourself to your team. This is how to get an advantage over the competition with a customer.

Really think about why you are good at what you do. What makes you different? What are the things that are always true about you, how you work, and why you are successful?

This information helps both parties get to the right outcome more quickly. I once interviewed with a CEO of a billion-dollar company for a COO position. Early in the interview, I told him, "Among other specific things we will talk about, when you get me, you will get an organization that functions better. That's just what I do. I pretty much can't help it. In any job I am in, I get the whole organization aligned and motivated to drive a clear business strategy."

He said, "Thanks for telling me that. That's not what I am looking for. I am basically looking for a sales manager, but I called it a COO role so that I would get higher-caliber candidates interested." Being clear about what is always true about me saved us both a lot of time, and I went on to find a job where getting the organization working was a critical factor.

Story: Game-Changing Initiatives

For an executive interview, you need to talk about game-changing initiatives, not just problem solving, managing teams, and delivering results. You need to have stories about how you got above the work and conceived of new opportunities or broader solutions to problems, and how you led and drove change in the organization to implement them and get the benefit. Here are some examples:

- **P&L Impact:** It's not that you ran marketing and generated leads. It's that you saw an opportunity in the market, and you proposed a new business initiative to go after it. You built an online channel and promotion engine, and you added significant incremental revenue to the business.

  It's not that you managed eighteen quarters of over-quota sales performance. It's that you built a brand new program to focus on strategic accounts and reorganized and trained the sales force to build relationships and deliver higher-value solutions, resulting in consistent, stronger-than-ever business growth.

It's not that you reduced the cost in IT. It's that you came up with a model to outsource specific functions and to upgrade the in-house talent in more strategic areas to enable faster time to market in your retail sales channels.

- **Process and Productivity Improvements:** It's not that you delivered product releases on time. It's that you rebuilt the management team when you saw that there were no processes or measures to make sure that product releases were aligned with business goals. And you pioneered a process improvement initiative across the organization, which improved quality and reduced product cycle time.

- **Organization and People Transformation:** You didn't just manage a team of 250 people. You restructured the organization to be more competitive and got them all aligned, on board, and reenergized. You kept them and motivated them when an acquisition caused you to discontinue a product line they had worked on for years. You were able to get them focused on the future opportunity and executing well with very little attrition.

Story: I Get the Scope

Managing twenty people is very different from leading two hundred people, and very different from organizational development for two thousand people. As we talked about in chapter 6, The Level Dilemma, you must understand what the leadership and managerial tasks are at the higher level, and you need to be really clear about what you will do, emphasize, value, and measure.

I remember once interviewing a really talented guy for a VP-level position. I suspected he could do the job, but he didn't have even one story or idea of what he would do that was at the right level. He didn't get the job because he kept talking about issues and opportunities from the perspective of his current level. He talked about how to lead a team like his current team, which was a much smaller, narrower team than the VP role would manage. I needed him to step up in the interview and talk at the scope of the new job.

What are the new indicators of success? What are the levers? What outcomes will you expect? How will you motivate your leadership team? How will you hold them accountable? What culture do you want to create? Where will you innovate? Where will you change the game first? How will you recruit people? What will you look for? How will you measure and improve productivity? How will you develop talent?

KEY INSIGHT: *Make sure you consider the answers to these questions at the new level and test yourself to ensure that your answers are different from your answers at your current level.*

Be prepared to proactively discuss your personal leadership strategy as well as your philosophy and approach on some of these topics.

Do Start Doing the Job

If there is any secret weapon in your quest to be the one who wins the job, it's to start doing the job before you are in it—not just similar tasks at this level, but the actual job.

Do your first month on the job before you get to the interview. Learn everything you can about the company, the people, the competition, the customers, and the market. Go into your interview with your deliverables:

- An assessment of the current state

- Challenges and opportunities

- A desired outcome description of the organization's future state

- A straw-man list of strategic priorities

- Key initiatives to fill the gap

- A list of problems to be solved

- A list of key communications necessary to support the work

The underlying thought in all of this is that you don't want to be talking about what you have done in your old role as much as how you will *do* the job you are interviewing for, and what you have *already done* for the job. To be convincing, the most powerful thing you can do is just start doing the job.

This gives you three advantages:

1. It is a great way to demonstrate that you get the requirements and you are able to work at the right level. You are showing you are not going to get lost in the detail and will focus on those elements of the role that will have the biggest impact on the business.

2. It shows them how you think and work. It's hard to know people just from an interview. Your work will give them a way to really understand how you will perform. This will make them comfortable about what they'll get if they get you. That gives you a leg up.

3. You will already have added value to their business. If you do this well, they will see you in the job, doing the job, and will get hooked on the work you are doing. So they will want you to keep doing it!

During the interview, present your work, ask questions about it, and get feedback. It's pretty easy to work this in. Sure, you have to answer their questions, but not for the whole time.

When someone asks, "How would you handle this?" or "What have you done?" you can say, "Well actually, I did an assessment of your business and I found two key areas that I believe need significant attention. Could I ask you some questions about that to see if I got this right?" and so on.

Do Bring in External Feedback

Do your homework: gather some external commentary, feedback, and review of the business. You will appear very smart by bringing an outside voice into your evaluation of the business. They are not hearing this from most of the other internal candidates who are coming to the interview with an internal view. They are not hearing this from all of the external candidates either—it's a real chance to stand out.

So make sure you do this for both internal and external interviews. This will be expected of you if you are an external candidate, but if you are an internal candidate it will really stand out.

There are good reasons for bringing in external feedback:

- It makes you come across like an industry expert.

- Having information about customer, competitor, analyst, and media reactions to the business shows that you know where the real drivers for the business are.

- Having a broad set of external inputs shows that you have a strong personal network that you can use for other things.

I've done this for every executive job I have ever won; I have started doing the job ahead of time and brought in significant external information. It is a compelling and useful platform to base your interview on.

Do Show External Influence, Recognition, and Support

Another key factor for qualifying and standing out for a big job is to have broad influence and to be recognized externally for what you achieve.

- Instead of being known internally for supporting revenue generation, demonstrate that you have had direct field and front-end experience; even better, if you can, is to show new revenue streams that you created.

- Instead of just being known internally as a good communicator, be seen as a media-savvy spokesperson, have a public persona, and put forth a point of view in the industry by speaking and publishing.

- Instead of simply being well connected internally, show that you have a very large personal network of customers, partners, and peers. Your external network far outweighs your internal one.

For a big role, something impressive had better come up for the hiring team during an online search. If not, you need to start some media work; begin publishing and spending time outside your company. Even if what you want is a top job in your own company, this type of public presence and validation of your position in the industry will put you head and shoulders above the competition.

The bigger the role, the broader your influence needs to be. As a top executive your impact needs to be on a much broader and more external stage. You need to prove that you know how to impact business growth and transformation internally and externally in a big way, if you want a big job.

* * *

The Hard (and Important) Part

It can be really hard to let go of all of your best stories and successes and realize that they are no longer impressive. In fact, in the context of the new bigger job, they will hold you back. It's painful to let them go. You've built your reputation on this great work and these impressive outcomes—it's where your confidence comes from. You need to accept that they don't count for much anymore.

As you move up, not only does no one care how hard you worked, but they don't even care about the business outcomes you drove, because those business outcomes are at too low a level. They don't qualify you for the bigger job.

You need to connect at a higher level. You need to get really clear about what bigger transformations and business outcomes matter in the new role and show that you have the experiences and network that support driving them.

You'll need to invent new successes and new stories that are worthy of your future.

Next . . . You will never get the job
if you are not on "the List."

20. Getting on "the List"

There Is Always a List; You Need to Get on It

"The List" is like the pot of gold at the end of the rainbow for your CONNECT Better efforts.

For any good job there is a list of people that the decision maker will choose from. If you are not on the List, you won't get the job.

It doesn't matter how open the decision-making process appears to be. If you are not on the List, you will not be considered. So you need to figure out how the List gets created in your environment—and get onto it.

Who Does the Decision Maker Listen To?

When determining how to get on the List, this is your most critical piece of information. An executive will really listen to some of her direct reports but not others. She often listens to her assistant. She will listen to some of her peers. She may listen to her partner. She may listen to key customers.

You need to do some archaeology to determine this—the real answer is never found on the formal organization chart. This is equally important whether you are going for a job inside your company or externally. You need to find out who, specifically, the decision maker listens to.

You can start with Human Resources. Sometimes HR is in the inner circle, sometimes they are not, but they usually have a pretty good idea of who is. Simply ask people, "Who does she go to for input? Who does she listen to?" It's remarkable that for something that seems so mysterious and untouchable, you can start to form a pretty accurate picture if you just ask!

The decision maker always has an inner circle of people she listens to. When there is a job to be filled, she will ask that inner circle: "Who should we consider for this role?" The candidates they recommend become "the List." You need to get yourself on the List, or you have no chance.

Develop a Relationship with Someone in the Inner Circle

When I got my first really big job, running sales and marketing worldwide for a $1 billion business, I would not have been on the List if it hadn't been for a mentor who put me on it. The hiring manager did not know me at all, and my background was very different from that of all the other candidates he was considering. He had been thinking of the role in a different way. My resume would never have made the cut. There is no way I would have gotten the opportunity to interview on my own if my mentor had not gotten me on the List.

Once I got on the List, I was able to compete for the job, and I won it. During the interview process, I was able to prove my capabilities and why my background would allow me to be even more successful than my competition.

But if my mentor hadn't said, "You need to interview Patty too," I would never have been considered.

Having a mentor who can get you on the List is the most powerful way to do it, but sometimes you don't have time for that. An opportunity comes up and you need to jump.

Do Some Outreach

Sometimes you need to create opportunities to meet and impress people in the inner circle. Refrain from trying a hard sell or asking them to do things for you. This can backfire.

A simple way to approach them is to send them an email: "I understand this job is coming open. I'm really interested in it. I know your team will be connected with this person. Would you mind sharing what you think is most important for this role?"

You can also write a short article that demonstrates your expertise on an area key to this job. Or share some recommendations about which outcomes you would drive if you were in the role, and ask for feedback.

If you get a meeting, great! Ask insightful questions, listen, offer suggestions about how you will do the job, and close by saying that you plan to apply for the job. By doing this, you will make your intentions known, and if you succeeded at making a good impression, when the decision maker asks his circle, "Who should I be considering for this job?" you've got a shot. If your name is mentioned, they might say, "Yes, I know that person; you should consider him." If you made a really good impression, they may inject you into the process proactively.

Even if you don't get the meeting, you will have made your name and intentions known, and you will stand a much better shot at getting the interview than if you had remained invisible.

Don't Be Annoying

It's so very important to not be annoying. That can get you on a different list! You need to approach these meetings with the posture of adding value, understanding, being helpful, and not overselling or asking for too much.

This is another reason to develop mentor relationships with people whom your decision makers listens to far ahead of time. This is an easy, nonannoying way to get on the List when it comes up. And you won't have to awkwardly force the issue with someone new at the last minute.

Make Your Claim

Tell people what role you want. Let people know. If you think a new role needs to be created that you should fill, talk about it. This can work well in your current company because you know the opportunities and the gaps, and people know you. But I've even seen this work—and seen it done very boldly—by someone who gets a meeting at a new company they are interested in. They go in and say convincingly, "You need this problem solved; hire me and I'll do it."

If you never stake a claim and stand up for what you want, people won't guess, and they won't automatically associate your general greatness with a specific role.

If you are a high performer, people will expect that you will be moving up, so make it clear with your boss and your mentors specifically what you are after.

If you want to run a global services organization, and you are in a regional support organization, no one will think about you for the bigger role unless you have made it clear that that is your aspiration. Even your mentor may not know to recommend you for the role if you've never mentioned it.

In this example, you can see how useful it is to have a mentor who is in a global services role herself. You will have spent months talking and learning about it from her. She will clearly identify you as someone who is targeting a global services role. She will be motivated to help you. She is likely to be in the circle of people who are asked, "Who should we consider for this global services role?"

Get Experience

You need to be thought of and credible as someone in the bigger role. Even if a mentor gets you onto the List, if you are not a credible candidate, you won't get any further than that.

There are always a few high-potential people who are interviewed but not really considered. Companies do this to get to know their high performers and give them a chance to practice interviewing for bigger jobs. So they are on a sublist of people to watch, but not quite on the List of people actually being considered.

To make sure you are on the real list, you need to get experience in the job before you are in it, as we talked about in chapter 18, The Experience Paradox. That way you get useful experience and people *see* you in the job.

KEY INSIGHT: *The obvious benefit is that you will have real experience to talk about in your interview, but the other key benefit is that it helps you make the credibility jump.*

Getting experience on the job before you are in it gets people associating you with being in that job and working at that level. It gets them thinking about you in your desired role, giving you the credibility you need to win the job.

* * *

The Hard (and Important) Part

This concept of getting on the List is probably the most political topic I have raised.

You really do need to get your name out there and position yourself clearly in the place you want to be—like a political campaign.

This doesn't have to be an ugly or shallow effort, but you do have to promote yourself and your intentions with the people who can put you on the List. If you do this based on a steady record of excellent results, if you run your "campaign" in such a way that you are always giving more to your network than you are taking, it won't feel ugly or disingenuous. It won't feel too political.

If you want the big job, this outreach is a necessary part of the process. Get comfortable with it.

Next . . . We are at the end of the model. Now it's time to take action, decide what you really want, and make your work fit into your life in such a way that your life works.

Part 4

GO!

Make Your Work, and Your Life, Work

Make the right tradeoffs on purpose.
Get better at enjoying your life while
you are earning a living.

21. Work and Life: Be Better at Both

Work and Life Do Not Have to Compete as Much as You Think

It's important to step back and really think about what you want—not just your next job or your next house or your next trip. If you fast-forward twenty years and then look back, what will make you feel good about how you spent those twenty years? Real success is personal. It's not what anyone else wants for or expects from you.

Often people have trouble coming up with the answer to the question, "What does success really mean to you?" They don't have a particular goal. If you want to be a CEO by a certain age, or have a particular amount of money in the bank by a certain date, those are fairly concrete goals. But if you don't have really clear goals, how do you answer the question?

Your True Desired Outcome

Try thinking more generally about what you want to make come true in your life. Do you want to have adventures? Do you want to pass your values on to your children? Do you want to spend lots of time in nature? Do you want to be with really smart people? Really think about what you want to make sure happens in your life. That is the root of your true desired outcome.

Your true desired outcome is true to you. It's not what it is "supposed to be." It's not what your family or your colleagues think you should be doing. It is not all about work. It is about work and life and what you really want to make happen overall in your life.

Why is this useful? Because plans don't work. It is impossible to plan a sequence of steps in your career over ten or twenty years. But establishing a true desired outcome for your career and life is really helpful. Here's why.

You Avoid Wasting Time

The more clear you can be about your true desired outcome, the more clear you can be in the moment about whether or not you are wasting your time. You can ask, "Is my role building capital to achieve my desired outcome or degrading it?" It lets you make judgments at different points to see if what you are doing in the moment is helpful, neutral, or damaging to achieving your desired outcome in life.

The great benefit of having this defined is not that it prescribes a specific plan, but that, in tough and confusing times, it gives you a picture to fall back on—a vision of what all this effort and activity is supposed to amount to.

As an example, I once left a job that I loved. I loved my boss; my boss loved me. I loved my team; my team loved me. We were doing great. But one morning I woke up and thought to myself, "Damn! I am starting to waste time here. If I spend any more time in this lovely job, I am missing an opportunity to build the career capital and the experience I need to become a CEO."

I ended up going after what turned out to be the worst job I've ever had. It was a turnaround situation in a failing business where everyone was angry. For the first six months I was completely miserable, but because this job required me to be in charge of strategy, marketing, and sales generation globally, it was exactly the kind of experience I needed to become a CEO.

So, as hard as it was, I made the tradeoff between a happy, fun job, and the experience I needed to attain my desired outcome. I felt good about it because I made the choice on purpose, and it helped me survive the low points.

We ultimately turned the business around and it became a great job—in fact, it was my last job before becoming a general manager. But I never would have left my happy job if I had not had a desired outcome defined, causing me to assess my situation and question it.

This choice to move from a happy but safe to an ugly but high-impact job serves as a great example of how having defined my big desired outcome allowed me to make decisive and effective choices and tradeoffs in my career. The CEO outcome served me very well for many years. Ultimately, after achieving that goal, I decided to incorporate more life-oriented goals into my big-picture desired outcome. I realized that I had a broader desired outcome than operating as the head of a single company.

The Hard Part—There *Is* Conflict

There is inherent conflict in fitting your job into your life. Say you want to have a big career and make a lot of money, or make a difference in the world, *but* you want to spend time with your family and enjoy your life outside of work too. You feel like these are in conflict.

Or you really don't enjoy your work and really just want to be spending your time doing other things.

Both of these situations result in constantly questioning: Am I doing the right thing?

I know people who second-guess themselves for years and years, either feeling guilty about working a lot, feeling resentful that their success is limited by their family obligations, or feeling depressed that their job is sapping all the life out of their life.

Unless you are already independently wealthy, you need to be earning an income to pay the bills and fund your fun. But you don't need to let the fact that you need to earn money ruin your whole life.

Many people feel unhappy because they try to optimize everything at once, and the resulting failure to do so feels bad. In reality, having a desired outcome defined is not magically going to eliminate the need for a paycheck or give you double the time to do what you want to do in work and life. But it does let you make decisions and tradeoffs on purpose. And that not only makes it feel a lot better and less stressful, but also helps you to

- Make much better judgments about how you are spending your time and whether it is amounting to anything—so you can proactively avoid wasting time, stuck in a job that is not helping you.

- Make some tradeoffs on purpose, so you feel like you are more in control of the outcome and not questioning yourself all the time.

Make Tradeoffs on Purpose

The clearer you can be about what *you* really want in your work and your family life, the more easily you can make tradeoffs on purpose. And you can make different tradeoffs at different times.

Let's face it. There will be times in your career that you will cancel your vacation to deal with a launch or a customer issue, and other times that you won't. If you are clear about your outcome, you can make those choices on purpose—different priorities at different times.

You can sometimes work "too much" for good reasons, and at other times you can pass up work opportunities in favor of family. And along the way you can prioritize small things that keep you connected with your family, even if you can't spend as much time as you want with them sometimes. When you make choices for reasons that serve your desired outcome, you feel much more in control and much more satisfied.

You can also recruit your family to be on your side if you share your thoughts about what all this work and money is for. What is it amounting to? This shared understanding of your true desired outcome can relieve you of huge amounts of stress.

Balance, No—Purpose, Yes

I'm sorry, but balance just doesn't work. Particularly if you are ambitious. You are going to work very hard and focus on your career at the expense of the rest of your life from time to time.

However, building your career and letting your life go to hell does not work either. The trick is, if you want to do better at either work or life, you need to get better at both.

If this seems impossible, just think about it this way. If your work is making you miserable, you won't be good to your family, and if your family is making you miserable, you won't be as good at your work. The only way out of this is to force yourself to get incrementally better at both.

If your family is a source of strength, you can apply even more energy to your work. And if you are handling your job with ease and grace, you will have more energy to be good to your family.

Don't Make It Such a Competition

Try to think of work and life as mutually reinforcing instead of in competition.

If you are doing great in your career but your family is unhappy or your life has no life in it, you have the constant stress of causing disappointment, or outright arguing, and feeling guilty about your family and time outside of work. That energy drain is keeping you from fully optimizing your career.

One of my favorite stories is about a colleague, a very ambitious hard-working woman in her thirties. Her husband is a gifted school teacher. She is investing a lot of time and energy in building her career, and her husband is doing good in the world with his teaching and supporting her every step of the way.

On the day when a new blockbuster movie came out, he called her at work around noon and said, "I'd really like to go see the movie today on opening day." She looked at her workload and said, "Sorry, I have to work late." Instead of being disappointed, getting upset, and giving her a hard time, here is what he did. He said, "The last showing is at 9:30 p.m. If we meet at the movie theater, can you make it?" After she agreed, here is what he did: He cleaned the whole house and packed her a dinner. He put it in a fancy shopping bag with a silk scarf over it, so the movie theater would not see that it was food and would let her bring it in.

That is a picture of a couple whose life and work are both working!

Don't Zero Out

There is finite time in the day, week, and month. Even if you are optimizing for work, it is important to not let the rest of your life zero out completely.

> **KEY INSIGHT:** *There is a much bigger difference between doing nothing and doing something small, than between doing something small and something big.*

If there is something you want to be doing and you're not doing it at all, the feeling of zero feels really bad. But the feeling of something, even if it's small, stops that really bad feeling of zero.

People tend to set themselves up to think if they can't do the big thing, then life is bad. If you love to travel the world, but your work or family prevents it, then you are miserable. But why not go away for a weekend somewhere once or twice a year?

Or if you really crave some peace and quiet and time to think, but can't get away, go sit in your car for fifteen minutes every day.

There is a huge difference between zero and something. You can always do something.

I was talking to a very senior consultant whose job kept him on the road virtually all the time, including weekends, when he would travel to and from clients. He felt like he was getting no time at all with his family. The big thing he wanted was to spend lots of evenings and weekends with his family. That was just not going to happen in this job. So he told his firm that one weekend a quarter would be his. The difference between zero and something makes a big psychological difference for you and your family.

Later he made another career choice, to optimize the time he spent with his family.

You can't optimize everything all at once, but you can make sure you don't zero out.

You can easily trade off some work time for some life time. These days, for an increasing number of people, it is very easy to work outside the office. Tell your boss that you are going to come it at 11:00 on Wednesday, and take your partner out to breakfast. Trade a weekday to go on a school trip, then do some work on a weekend.

It's Up to You to Be OK

Part of your job is to figure out how to not be fully consumed and burned out. The better you get at your job, the more you can get done in a shorter amount of time with less effort and energy. You'll then have more time and energy to do things outside of work.

You need to take responsibility to make time to do the things over and above your job description that will make you successful, including claiming some time to get better at your home life. Your company wants you to have a good life that you enjoy. They know they will get more out of you at work if you are happy outside of work.

Next . . . What it's really like to be an executive

22. Executive Confessions

Do You Really Want the Executive *Job*
or Just the Executive *Pay*?

I included this chapter in the GO section because there are some things about being a big executive that are worth considering as you get there. I wanted to make sure that everyone knows that it can be scary but that's OK. It's not supposed to be not-scary.

Being a big executive has moments of greatness—and ugliness. Knowing who you really are helps a lot to set you up for success and protect you through the hard parts. Being true to who you really are and bringing others along with you will help you succeed in such a way that you can still like your life.

Being a Big Executive: The Money

Big executives in big companies can make a lot of money. I'm not only talking about the multimillion dollar annual incomes of the top people we all hear about in all the business media. But if you are a mere-mortal big executive—

either a few steps down in a really big company, or a big cheese in a smaller, big company—you can still make $1 million-plus per year.

If this is your desire, first you need to get one of these jobs! This requires managing your career with this intention over time. You can use this book as a roadmap to get there. Build your plan to DO Better, LOOK Better, and CONNECT Better to win one of these jobs.

Being a Big Executive: The Dark Side

These jobs are *hard*. The tools in this book will not magically take all the gut-wrenching challenge out of your executive job, but they will help you make choices on purpose about what kinds of pain are worth it. They will also help you to tune your job over time to suit your strengths and values, so you eliminate as much of the aggravation as possible.

Here's how it goes: from my own experience and discussing this with others, basically, you get paid the first $250,000 annually for your brains and your results.

The second $250,000, you get paid for frustrating, time-wasting, disheartening big company slowness and bureaucracy, needing to defend your honor and your budget constantly, and frequent changes of direction causing embarrassment and rework—basically, to deal with your allocation of corporate crap.

Anything north of half a million a year is the hazard pay for the company acting like it owns you, letting you know your time is not your own, and finding seemingly laser-targeted ways to torture you. If you are not a morning person, there will be 6 a.m. staff meetings every day; if you are not a night person, you will be given responsibility for a team on the other side of the globe and have regular meetings at 10 p.m.; if you hate international travel, you will get a project to live in Asia for a year—you get the idea. There will be people in positions of power who will grate against your values in painful ways, and you'll be stuck with them. Expect this, and be prepared to take it in stride. You need to find your own way to be OK with whatever it is (all the money helps, by the way—if you walk away to stop the pain, they stop paying you!).

You will find that you get to spend about a third of your time on what the job description says you should be doing—growing the business. The balance of your time will be divided among defense, communications, and wasted time:

- Defense: Justifying budgets and strategies, dealing with peer attacks, customer escalations.

- Communications: Representing the business to partners, customers, industry analysts, media, and Wall Street. Regular internal communications to keep employees informed, aligned, and motivated is also critical.

- Wasted time: Lots of meetings, travel, dealing with HR problems, reorganizations, strategy changes, budget cuts, and rework.

Once you are in the job, in addition to executing well, you will need to have a fairly constant focus on building and maintaining your personal credibility—the LOOK Better part. If you let this go for too long, you will slide into obscurity and lose relevance and organizational power. Also, building and feeding connections and networks of support along the way is fundamental. CONNECT Better. This is the positive side of politics. You will not survive without this. You will also certainly encounter the negative side of politics, so you need to be prepared. Building credibility and relevance is a good offense. It is also your best defense.

If leading a very large organization does not seem very interesting to you, or these downsides seem horrific, or both, you will struggle in an executive role. Is what you really want the executive *job*, or do you just want the executive *pay*?

If, however, these challenges seem like a doable reality, or even a fun challenge, an executive job could be a good fit for you.

Toxic Bosses

I think it's important to include a note on toxic bosses. You may encounter one on the way up. These are the narcissists and bullies. These are the people who degrade and demean. These are the people who fly into a rage with little or no provocation.

Or sometimes these are the bosses whose transgressions are ones of omission. They are useless. They hold you back because they are incompetent or checked out, or they won't deal with reality. They put or leave you in terrible situations with no support.

If you have a toxic or useless boss who is damaging you and your career, you need to get out. It's not worth your time, your health, or the money that lured you into this in the first place. One of the themes throughout this book is that you need to take control of making the right things happen in your career. Sometimes the thing you need to take control of is getting out from under a bad boss.

Being an Executive: The Fun Part

It can be very exciting and satisfying to have a big organization and a big responsibility. It can be very rewarding to drive an organization that has a material impact on the company's performance and contributes something significant to the market. You will have personal responsibility to drive revenue and manage costs, uncover and create new business opportunities, set and lead the organizational culture, and represent the business to the world at large.

Some people thrive on leading very large organizations. If you enjoy either driving results on a very large scale or being responsible for the livelihood of thousands of people, or if you like the idea of "being somebody important" (at least in your company/industry), then these things, in addition to the big money, will help offset the bad parts—particularly if either the specific experience or the money or both directly serve your long-term big desired outcome.

It's OK to Be Terrified

In fact, if you are terrified, you are doing it right! I was lucky to have mentors and coaches share this with me, and I want to share it with you.

All executives feel at certain points like they are in over their heads, don't know what do to, aren't doing a good enough job, and are going to be "found out"—particularly when they start a new job. If you want your career to advance to the big executive level and you are terrified doing it, congratulations—you are doing it right!

By the way, if you are very talented and motivated you will find yourself both younger and less well paid than both your peers and the people that work for you. One sign that you are on a fast track is that you spend most of your career at the bottom of the pay curve, because you get promoted too quickly to ever climb up a pay curve for a particular level.

Part of the success formula is being willing to take these leaps and throw yourself into situations where you don't know much or where you could be challenged as inexperienced. You need to trust yourself to be smart enough, and then you need to learn really fast!

My Personal Job Fears

The first six months of every big new job I ever had were really hard. I had to step into the role and inspire confidence as a leader before I had it myself. I had to make decisions and get work done before I knew what I was doing. And I had to spend every extra waking moment learning as fast as I could.

But so does everybody at these levels. This is the phase that turns some people into beloved leaders and others into tyrants. The tyrants will never admit, to themselves or others, any weakness of any kind, and they will work very hard on their "I know everything" and "I am in charge" façade.

My approach was different. My approach was what I describe in this book. First, I would reach out to my staff as humans, make a respectful, personal connection with them, and let them continue to run their part of the business as I got educated. I listened to them a lot. I learned at every moment. Every time I heard a word I didn't know, I would either ask or jot it down on my "things I don't know" page and find out later.

I remember one time in the biggest job I ever took on: although I knew the big picture of where I wanted to take the organization, the major problems that I wanted to fix, and the big opportunities I wanted to go after, it was all hugely generalized. I had no idea how to actually do it. I was also a novice in the content of the business. The only thing I was expert in was leading. Other than that I was pretty lost!

So in parallel to developing relationships, I initiated a business planning process. This had several benefits. It gave me time to learn. It helped me learn. It gave me time to get to know the players, and who I was going to bet the future on, and what their unique talents were so I could make sure to get them into the right roles. It also gave me, for the first couple of months, a ready answer to many pointed questions that I had no idea how to answer: "That will be decided once we have completed the business planning process."

But underneath all of this, I was scared. I did business reviews with every group—every product team, every service team, every regional team. I asked them what was working and not working, and what they thought we should do differently. Six weeks went by. I had done dozens of reviews, and I had not heard a single thing repeated. I felt like I was in way over my head and that I was failing. "This should be making more sense by now. . . . I should know what to do. . . . I'm not qualified. . . ."

I was very lucky to have a mentor in whom I could confide at this point, who said to me, "Patty, it *is* new. New is stressful. It is supposed to be. It's *new.* Give yourself a break. This is how you are supposed to feel. And you will see that it will all snap into focus at some point soon."

And about two weeks later, it did. Suddenly, everything I was hearing fit into a big picture that I could see. It was in focus. I ended up doing a large-scale transformation of this business, building an amazing management team, winning over the organization, and growing the business ahead of the market.

It's OK to Be Scared—It's Not OK to Be Paralyzed by It

You are scared because you have made a leap. Leaps are scary. This happens to everyone who has made a big leap. If you find yourself in this situation, heed the words of my mentor. You'll be fine. Listen a lot and get help from your mentors.

Things You Are Crappy At

As an executive you should have a clear view of what you are bad at and hate doing. It may be tracking execution; it may be internal employee communications; it may be that you are not a visionary. Know what your strengths are and know what you are bad at and recognize whether you are missing a strength that is putting you or the company at risk or causing you to fail at something important.

Then Stop Worrying about It and Get Someone Else to Do It

If you are not getting around to employee communications, assign someone to poll the organization, write you a script, and schedule you to do it. If you are not good at tracking execution, find someone that thrives on process and detail and give them a position on your staff to do this for you.

Remember, your job is to see that the work gets done, not to do all the work yourself. You are a human; you are supposed to be bad at some things. Don't try to cover these up or just accept the fact that you are failing at them. You are the boss. It is up to you to change and build the organization that will thrive and deliver with you as the leader. This is *your* organization. This will be a different organization than one that would thrive and deliver well with someone else as the leader.

Bluffing

Everyone is bluffing. We all know "our stuff," but every executive job puts us in situations that require us to know more than "our stuff." Executives in the back of their mind often feel like they are going to get found out. *Everyone is going to discover that I don't know everything. I'm a fraud!*

Successful executives are masterful at coming across as confident and informed, but it is not because they know everything. It's because they are good at bluffing.

There will always be a press conference or a customer meeting where you will get a question that you have no idea how to answer. You will be faced with decisions of what to do in a crisis, and you won't have a clue.

The path to success is not to make sure you know everything. Sure, you need accurate, deep knowledge about the key factors that drive your business. But you will never get to the point where you know the answer to every question. The fear of not knowing every detail about everything is one of the big hazards that gets you stuck, as we discussed in earlier chapters. The path to success is to retain your composure, make the best comment or decision you can with the data you have at the time, and rely on smart people around you to fill in as many gaps as possible.

One of the best ways to manage yourself in this situation is to get people focused on the desired outcome. When people are asking, "What should we do next?" or customers or media are asking, "What is your specific plan to solve this supply chain/architecture/product issue?" (and you have no idea what they are even talking about), you can say "Help me understand your motivation for asking that question. What is the business outcome you are most concerned about?" Then you can make a comment on the business outcome. You have taken the conversation to a smart and useful place, and you have successfully bluffed. Then you can take the question back to your team later.

When you see executives being interviewed and they seem to be evading the question, giving an answer to a different question, sometimes the reason is that the question takes them into an area that would reflect badly on the business—so they genuinely try to avoid it, for PR reasons—and sometimes it's because they just don't know the answer so they talk about something they do know!

Bluffing is just another example of why being an executive takes a fair amount of guts, and you need to be OK with the fact that from time to time you are going to be scared and way out of your comfort zone. That is a requirement of the job—get comfortable with it.

Loyalty Issues

If you are going to advance, you need to be willing to leave your team. It sounds pretty obvious, but this is something that can be really difficult. Imagine that you handpicked and built a team, and then the world changed and your company is now a horrible place to work.

You have a chance to move on to a big promotion in a better place. But you feel terrible about leaving your team in this unstable turmoil. What do you do?

You leave your team. You will feel guilty. They will miss you. You will miss them. But you move on. You tell them, "I admire and respect you greatly, and I will miss you terribly, but I need to make this decision for myself and my family. I will do everything I can do to help you in your careers moving forward." (I have done this myself a number of times.)

If you have treated them well along the way, they will be disappointed but not angry or resentful. Stepping up means leaving. If you can't deal with this, you can't step up.

Here's another way to look at this: if you are in a situation in which your whole team is at risk (including you), you may think your job is to stay to protect them for as long as possible. I have seen managers go down with the ship, and then they are no longer in a position to help anyone. *The ones who move on can sometimes hire people from their own team in their new role.* Even if that is not the case, you have far more power helping your former team get places if you are sitting in a position of power than if you are unemployed too. And you are also in a position to help a whole new team of people. Your net ability to help other people goes way up if you take care of yourself. If you lose your job out of loyalty to your team, you dramatically reduce your ability to help anyone.

It is OK to take care of yourself. If you feel guilty about it, try this. Match the amount of energy you spend worrying about and taking care of yourself with the amount of energy you spend doing things to worry about and take care of helping your team. That way you make sure you don't become a selfish, self-centered bastard. You are keeping yourself strong and taking care of them too.

Big Executives Are Not Smarter Than You

Sometimes it's hard to see where big executives come from. I hope the ideas you have seen in this book take some of the mystery out of how they got there. They don't start at the top. Most of them have been where you are and gotten there over time, some faster than others.

Successful, good leaders are very smart, and they have good emotional intelligence—but not necessarily more than you. What they have is more and different experience, a supportive network, and access to opportunities.

I remember the first time I got to sit in on an executive meeting where the executives were in the stratosphere compared to me. They were discussing a business challenge, and from the ideas they were putting out and the general level of discussion, I was amazed to conclude "These people are not smarter than me."

I can remember how at one and the same time I was really happy and really distressed—happy, because I thought: "I can get there. They are not smarter than me." And kind of horrified thinking: "You guys are running the company—I was hoping you were much smarter than me!"

How Tough Do You Need to Be?

Many people are concerned that you can't be a nice person and be a successful executive. We have all seen examples of assholes and narcissists who are hugely successful. Or, to be more polite, let's just say they are not nice.

Is there room for nice people at the top? Can you be a tough enough, business-minded executive and still be decent and kind to people?

Yes, you can. I learned this from a mentor I have had in my life since I was nineteen years old! He is an amazingly powerful businessman and a wonderful human being. He showed me it can be done. I have used his example as my model for the type of executive I wanted to be throughout my whole career.

As long as you demand rigorous accountability to the business and measure and manage performance accordingly, you can be nice to people.

Kind to people; hard on results.

Friendships at Work

Along these lines, I often get asked whether you can or should be friends with a boss or employee.

Yes, you can be friends, as long as the friendship does not keep you from being tough on accountability and results in the business.

If you are the kind of person who can keep those separate, friends at work are fine. But if you end up holding your friends less accountable, or not imposing consequences because they are friends, and this makes you uncomfortable, then don't make friends with employees.

If you don't seriously manage performance with employees who are friends, everyone will see that you are letting your friend get away with things. You will squander huge amounts of trust. People will accept your friendships as long as they see you being fair.

I personally have always had some employees who became friends, but I was always really clear on accountability. And when I was friends with my boss, I was still scared of not delivering, knowing I would not get any friend-related slack.

Nasty or Nice, You Need Support Either Way

As we have already discussed, no one can be successful on their own. They need to build a strong team and a strong network and get a lot of help. People get this support in one of two ways.

The nice way. You can build your support infrastructure by giving more than you take, by being respectful, including people, trusting them, and communicating well. You will build trust and loyalty, and people will help you. You will also be building an organization that will become more capable over time. You will be developing people who can step up to make big decisions and tradeoffs and run the business when you move on.

The nasty way. If you are an asshole, you build your support infrastructure with money and power. There will always be people who will be won over by money and power. You will stay squarely in charge, and your organization will do your work, but you won't be growing a capable organization beneath you. There will be no one to take over for you, which is fine for you because that is the way you want it.

The third way that doesn't work. You don't have money and power to offer *and* you are an asshole. Then you will not be able to build the support infrastructure you need to achieve big success. You'll just piss people off and get stuck.

Conclusion: the nice way works well, and it's more within your control anyway.

Grow Your People, Grow Your Business

You can build a powerful, capable, and growing team, and a successful business, and not be an asshole. The approach of DO Better, LOOK Better, and CONNECT Better I describe in this book is actually more controllable and predictable than trying to be a controlling, power-hungry leader. You create real value in the business and the people.

I am a firm believer that growing businesses come from growing people, and to be highly successful, you need to make the people supporting you successful too. It's not just about the money. Everyone wants to be effective, relevant, and satisfied in their work. Your career and business success will come from helping others achieve theirs.

Epilogue

I had a wonderful corporate executive career. I am very grateful for the mentors who pulled me up and the amazing teams who pushed me up.

These lessons for rising above the work, working where it counts, making sure it's recognized, and ensuring that your impact is far-reaching enough, were vital to my success. I hope that in this book I have conveyed a practical approach for you to apply these lessons of DO Better, LOOK Better, and CONNECT Better to your own career.

Work is hard, and nothing is perfect. I have had jobs that were just too miserable or impossible to survive because of a bad leader or toxic environment. Sometimes you just can't make it work. But I knew it was up to me to put myself in a position to thrive. So by keeping my long-term desired outcome in mind, and staying true to my natural strengths and values, I was able to aggressively transition between jobs, continue to build my career capital, and not have to sell my soul in the process.

When I look back on my career and what I accomplished, although I had many excellent business profit results to point to, what I am most proud of are the people, teams, and organizations I developed. The opportunity to open doors and give other people an opportunity to rise above the work and into bigger, better, and more satisfying careers, was the best part.

My big secret—how did I deliver such strong business results? Help people step up, and let them do great things.

Today, I work with CEOs and general managers to help whole organizations execute better, drive strategic change, and develop their leadership.

My Recipe for a Tuna Sandwich

First of all, the secret ingredient for a great tuna sandwich is tuna.

My husband is English and used to make sandwiches the English way, with just enough sandwich filling to subtly suggest the flavor of the sandwich and provide a minimal visual clue, a mere hint, of what type of sandwich it actually was.

When he made tuna sandwiches, he would make two sandwiches with one can of tuna and put the "leftover tuna" in the refrigerator (heavy sigh).

It was months later that he discovered the reason my tuna sandwiches were so good, when he caught me using two cans of tuna for two sandwiches. The secret ingredient is TUNA.

Either broil frozen tuna steaks and shred (best) or use one can of whole white albacore tuna in water and one can of chunk light tuna in water. Mix them together in a bowl. Chop up half an onion and add that, along with salt, black pepper, and as little mayonnaise as you need to moisten and hold the tuna together, but not so much that you are having mayonnaise with tuna.

Now add the juice of half a fresh lime and a small amount of mustard. Stir that in. Taste it and fuss with all the ingredients until you think it tastes great.

The other secret ingredient for a great tuna sandwich is the bread. Get a really nice loaf of ciabatta. Heat the oven to 250 degrees. Put the ciabatta in the oven until it gets crispy on the outside but is still soft and fluffy on the inside, about ten minutes.

Slice the bread across the middle so you have the top and bottom of the loaf in separate pieces. Put a little extra mustard on the bread, then pile on the filling. Make your sandwiches while the bread is warm and while a bottle of champagne is chilling.

As it turns out, the other secret ingredient for a great tuna sandwich is champagne.

Enjoy!

Resources

DO Better

Working the Right Way

- *The Leadership Pipeline*, by Ram Charan, Stephen Drotter, and James Noel (Jossey-Bass, 2001).

  This book provides a lot of additional insight about working at the right level.
- *Make More Time Workbook*: www.AzzarelloGroup.com/MakeMoreTime

  This downloadable workbook provides time management and optimization tools to help you focus on Ruthless Priorities and use your time better.

Self-Assessments

- *StrengthsFinder 2.0*, by Tom Rath (Gallup Press, 2007).

  This book comes with access to an online survey that can help you identify your natural strengths.
- *Myers-Briggs Profile*: www.MyersBriggsReports.com

  This widely used and very helpful personality profile can help you learn about how you relate to others.

LOOK Better

Standing Out

- *Build Your Personal Brand Workbook*: www.AzzarelloGroup.com/PersonalBrand

    This downloadable workbook provides step-by-step guidance and worksheets you can use to define and implement your personal brand.

Communicating

- *Bull Fighter*: www.FightTheBull.com

    This is a free online utility you can use to make sure your writing is clear, understandable, and free of bull. (There's also a book: *Why Business People Speak Like Idiots: A Bullfighter's Guide*, by Brian Fugere, Chelsea Hardaway, and Jon Warshawsky.)

- *Made to Stick*, by Chip and Dan Heath (Random House, 2007).

    This excellent book shows you how to construct high-impact, "sticky" communications.

CONNECT Better

Networking

- *Personal Networking Workbook*: www.AzzarelloGroup.com/AuthenticNetworking

    This downloadable workbook guides you through the steps of building and maintaining a strong personal and professional network.

- *Networking for People Who Hate Networking*, by Devora Zack (Berrett-Koehler, 2010).

GO!

Personal Action Plan

- *Career Year of Action Guide*: www.AzzarelloGroup.com/CareerYearAction

    Make the time to do some key tasks each month that will ensure you are actually making progress in your career, not just working really hard. If you need further help, you can download this step-by-step tool I've created, the *Career Year of Action Guide*. This guide stages out everything you've learned in this book in bite-sized chunks, over the course of a year.

Acknowledgments

I want to thank all the people who specifically took an interest in this book and gave me the encouragement, support, ideas, and feedback that kept me going. Thanks so much to Adam Bloom, Alan Shoap, Al Fasola, Andrew Binstock, Andy Burtis, Andy Sutton, Barbara Nelson, Ben Kiker, Bob Kaplan, Brian Kilcourse, Deepa Menon, Elaine Cummings, Eric Carrasquilla, Ericka Engelman, Hanna Walicki, Heidi Lorenzen, Hugh Lavery, Jacek Walicki, Jessica Kersey, Jessica Swank, Joanna Kulesa, Kerry Azzarello, Linda Beardsley, Marc McKenzie, Marlene Williamson, Melissa Boxer, Meta Mehling, Mike Ruck, Nick Goss, Nina Lytton, Paul Beiser, Phill Aranda, Resa Pearson, Richard Claeys, Richard Walker, Sandor Kovacs, Steve Diamond, Stuart Rakley, Suzanne Pherigo, Thomas Volk, Tiffany Tuell, and William Reeves.

Thanks also to the team at Ten Speed Press: editor Lisa Westmoreland, designer Katy Brown, publicist Kara Van de Water, marketing and publicity director Patricia Kelly, and marketing director Michele Crim.

I also want to thank my long-time professional mentors who made such a huge difference in my career and provided many of the lessons in this book: Al Fasola, Jim Davis, Bill Russell, Duane Zitzner, and Webb McKinney.

I want to say a special thank-you to Liz Saiz and Julie (Drake) Dubas for helping me get things done on a day-to-day basis and putting up with me when I was most in need of your help.

I also want to convey a big thank-you to Scott Jordan, Mike McGrorey, and Cathy FitzGerald for their brilliant and tireless help keeping our organizations executing well.

I suppose it is also worth noting that there have been a number of people throughout my career who inadvertently helped me to step up my game as a leader by being real bastards. You know who you are. . . .

Finally, thank you to the many, many colleagues who personally supported me through your hard work and loyalty in the businesses we were building, growing, or turning around. I am honored to have worked with you and so very grateful for your generosity and excellence.

About the Author

PATTY AZZARELLO became the youngest general manager at Hewlett-Packard at age thirty-three, ran a $1 billion software business at thirty-five, and became a CEO at thirty-eight (without turning into a self-centered, miserable jerk).

Whether leading massive business transformations or advising CEOs one to one, her insights, integrity, generosity, and down-to-earth approach have fused with her work to create life-changing impact on the careers of thousands of people in large and small companies across the world.

Patty has held leadership roles in general management, marketing, sales, and product development, including vice president and general manager of HP OpenView, president and CEO of Euclid Software, and chief marketing officer for Siebel Systems.

It's always been important to Patty to bring people up along with her. Her company, Azzarello Group, Inc. (www.AzzarelloGroup.com), is centered on this, working with companies to improve execution, drive strategic change, and develop their leaders.

Patty lives with her best friend–husband in a spectacular house atop the hills overlooking Carmel Valley, California. When she's not helping business leaders step up their game, you might find Patty scuba diving, cycling up the California coast, painting a picture, or singing in her rock band.

Join Patty in the business leadership conversation online:
Facebook: www.facebook.com/risebook
twitter: www.twitter.com/pattyazzarello

Index